you know you're in
new jersey when...

Some Other Books in the Series

You Know You're In Series

you know you're in
new jersey when...

101 quintessential places, people, events, customs, lingo, and eats of the garden state

Lillian Africano and Nina Africano

INSIDERS' GUIDE®

GUILFORD, CONNECTICUT
AN IMPRINT OF THE GLOBE PEQUOT PRESS

INSIDERS' GUIDE®

Text design by Linda R. Loiewski
Illustrations by Sue Mattero

Library of Congress Cataloging-in-Publication Data
Africano, Lillian.
  You know you're in New Jersey when— : 101 quintessential places, people, events, customs, lingo, and eats of the Garden State / Lillian Africano and Nina Africano. — 1st ed.
      p. cm. — (You know you're in series)
  Includes index.
  ISBN-13: 978-0-7627-3939-4
  ISBN-10: 0-7627-3939-8
  1. New Jersey—Miscellanea. 2. New Jersey—Description and travel—Miscellanea.
I. Africano, Nina. II. Title.
  F134.6.A35 2007
  974.9—dc22

                                                    2006027589

Manufactured in the United States of America
First Edition/First Printing

To all the great people who call New Jersey home—
you know who you are.

about the authors

Lillian Africano has written 16 books, including 3 best-selling novels (under a pen name) and hundreds of articles on everything from Antarctica to spas in Tuscany. A Jersey Girl by birth and by choice, Lillian loves to write about her home state—and when she cracks wise about its quirks and peccadilloes, she means it in a good way.

Coauthor, daughter, and fellow New Jerseyan **Nina Africano** writes regularly on golf and lifestyles for a variety of publications, including *Golf Digest* and Asbury Park Press. Together, she and Lillian are the authors of *Insiders' Guide to the Jersey Shore*.

to the reader

We've heard all the Jersey jokes—about how we talk funny; how we're home to wiseguys, crooked politicians, and toxic waste; and how we just ain't got no couth. Maybe you, our reader, have made a few of those jokes. We don't mind.

Joke if you like, but we know the facts. Jersey is rich, with the second-highest per capita income in the United States and the fifth-highest number of millionaires. We rank third in the number of Fortune 500 companies registered.

Jersey is smart. We spend more than anyone else on educating our kids—more than $10,000 per student—and we pay our teachers better than most states (we rank third). This investment pays off in the number of kids who go to college: One in three Jersey adults has a college degree.

(By the way, it was a Jersey Girl—Katharine Close of Spring Lake—who won the Scripps National Spelling Bee in 2006. Can *you* spell *Ursprache*? Katharine could.)

When it comes to history, few states have a better pedigree. The Declaration of Independence had five signers from Jersey: Abraham Clark, John Hart, Francis Hopkinson, Richard Stockton, and John Witherspoon.

We were the third state to join the union in 1787 and the first to sign the Bill of Rights. The 1776 New Jersey constitution was the first to grant women's suffrage, though some backward-looking politicians revoked it in 1807.

And for one brief, shining moment, our state capital was a serious candidate for capital of the United States. In fact, Trenton did serve as the working capital in 1784, but when it came to making the arrangement permanent, one man put the kibosh on the whole deal. It was George Washington, who owned some land in the Georgetown area and thought that it would be a better spot.

Never mind. Nation's capital or not, we have a lot to crow about. Jersey has recorded many important "firsts," but we have room to share only a few in this book.

As for the number of famous people we've produced, well, everyone knows about the eminent Frank Sinatra and Bruce Springsteen. Others prominent in show business or literature include Bud Abbott and Lou Costello, Count Basie, Jon Bon Jovi, David Copperfield, Sandra Dee, Danny DeVito, Michael Douglas, John Forsythe, Connie Francis, James Gandolfini, Alan

Ginsberg, Lauryn Hill, Whitney Houston, Brian Keith, Jerry Lewis, Norman Mailer, Ozzie Nelson, Jack Nicholson, Dorothy Parker, Joe Pesci, Joe Piscopo, Nelson Riddle, Jimmy Roselli, Paul Simon, Kevin Smith, Martha Stewart, Meryl Streep, Loretta Swit, John Travolta, Frankie Valli, Dionne Warwick, and Flip Wilson.

As you may have guessed by now, we're Jersey Girls who love our home state. It's a great place to live—and a lot of fun to write about.

you know you're in
new jersey when...
...comedy is classic

New Jersey has been home to a great many comedians over the years. Two who stayed out of politics and limited their antics to entertaining radio, film, and television audiences were Bud Abbott and Lou Costello.

Born Louis Francis Cristillo in Paterson, Costello often worked a little hometown humor into the duo's skits. William A. Abbott was an accidental Jersey boy; he was born to circus performers passing through Asbury Park.

The pair started in burlesque in 1936, with Abbott as the smooth-talking straight man trying to con the simple Costello. Abbott-and-Costello routines were strictly family fare, which transitioned easily to radio and film and later to television. After an appearance on the nationally broadcast *Kate Smith Radio Hour,* the pair were instant stars.

Their first film was *One Night in the Tropics* (1940), followed by *Buck Privates* in 1941. They made 36 films in all—some comedy classics, others formulaic but still funny, like *Abbott and Costello Meet Frankenstein*—before breaking up in 1957.

Abbott and Costello are best remembered for an old burlesque gag called "Who's on First?" Featured in *The Naughty Nineties* (1945), the sketch has Abbott trying to explain the strange nicknames of baseball players to a confused Costello with this famous line: "Who's on first, What's on

Abbott and Costello:

These Jersey-born comedians entertained America from the Depression era through the 1950s.

second, and I Don't Know is on third." Translated into more than 30 languages, "Who's on First?" got the comedians featured in the Baseball Hall of Fame Museum in Cooperstown, NY.

Lou Costello died in 1959. On March 6, 2006, the 100th anniversary of his birth, Governor Jon Corzine proclaimed a statewide Lou Costello Day. A bronze statue located at Cianci and Ellison Streets in Paterson portrays the comedian with his signature baggy pants and bowler hat, carrying a baseball bat. Fans also will find Abbott and Costello memorabilia displayed in the Paterson Museum (973–881–3874).

Abbott, who died in 1974, was honored posthumously at the 2006 Garden State Film Festival.

you know you're in
new jersey when...

... it's definitely *not* Granada you see, just Asbury Park

Clever Cole Porter was probably not the first, and certainly not the last, to get a laugh out of a Jersey put-down. But back in 1937, when he wrote "At Long Last Love" and asked the musical question "Is it Granada I see or only Asbury Park?" this thriving seaside resort had fine hotels, good restaurants, and a busy boardwalk lined with stands. The tuxedo set came from New York and Philly to see headliners like Artie Shaw, Glenn Miller, and the Marx Brothers at Asbury's oceanfront Paramount Theater and Convention Hall.

But as Asbury and other Jersey Shore beach towns became more and more popular, wealthy visitors moved on to more exclusive destinations like Palm Beach and the Hamptons.

Though less glamorous, Asbury Park continued to be a busy family resort through the 1950s and 1960s. Locals and day-trippers still remember the rides, cotton candy and frozen custard, skee ball in the arcades, and wall-to-wall people strolling the mile-long boardwalk.

Social unrest in the 1970s led to a long economic decline for Asbury, a period captured in Woody Allen's moody, black-and-white *Stardust Memories* and later, in the stark and depressing Robert De Niro film *City by the Sea*. For years it seemed like the only places still open in Asbury were music

haunts like the Stone Pony, most famous as the proving ground for Bruce Springsteen and the E Street Band.

Finally came a real estate boom loud enough to rumble through Asbury Park, whose lovely Victorian homes in desperate need of restoration and vacant commercial spaces attracted buyers from New York and Philadelphia. House prices are now triple what they were just a few years ago, and 10 times what they were in the late 1980s. The Main Street whitewashed windows and vacant stores that Springsteen lamented in "My Hometown" are now chic boutiques, trendy restaurants, and loft spaces.

Asbury Park:

After a long period of decline, this seaside resort is trendy again.

you know you're in
new jersey when...
...you've come a long way, baby

There's something about being down the Shore that makes people want to strut their stuff, which is great, because there seems to be no shortage of pageants to parade in—check out the Miss Crustacean Hermit Crab Beauty Contest and Miss Gay New Jersey competition (see pages 57 and 58).

But long before it was acceptable for decent citizens to make a spectacle of themselves, proud parents loved to show off their adorable children, and the place to do it was the Asbury Park Baby Parade. First held in the summer of 1890 and led by city founder James Bradley, the event drew 200 children; the grand prize was a baby carriage.

Ten years later, about 500 children participated, representing every state but two. Dressed up in colorful costumes and accompanied by their mothers, they marched or were pushed in elaborately decorated carriages, passing in review before the judges as Arthur Pryor, the city's famous bandmaster, conducted his orchestra.

The event grew into a three-day children's carnival and drew as many as 100,000 spectators, including two presidents, Theodore Roosevelt and Woodrow Wilson. It included elements drawn from Shakespeare's *A Midsummer Night's Dream* and much pomp and pageantry.

Asbury Park Baby Parade:

The granddaddy of all beauty pageants, this event was established in 1890 and revived in 2005.

Thomas Edison's film of the 1904 parade (catalogued in the Library of Congress) shows boys dressed as soldiers and sailors marching in groups; girls dressed in Oriental costumes riding in horse-drawn floats, and mothers pushing elaborately decorated carriages.

Except for the Depression and war years, the Baby Parade continued until 1949. A version of it reappeared in 1973 and lasted until 1981. In July 2005, with Asbury Park's renaissance in progress, the event was revived, once again featuring adorable tykes from newborns to toddlers. In keeping with the times, the winners in each category now get a modeling contract as well as assorted goodies and an official Asbury Park Baby Parade photo.

3

Atlantic City, once home to high-diving horses, Miss America, and midget boxing, is a day-tripper's paradise, drawing more than 33 million visitors a year. The A.C. Convention and Visitors Authority estimates that one-quarter of America's population lives within a day's drive of this Shore city. For over a century folks have been coming to stroll on the boardwalk (see page 13), and now they come to the casinos hoping to land one of the well-advertised mega-jackpots.

Ringing slot machines and flashing lights describe a variety of exotic themes—the Far East at Trump's Taj Mahal, ancient Rome at Caesar's, and the Old West at Bally's Wild, Wild West. They share the limelight with an attraction that perfectly complements A.C.'s nothing-is-too-outlandish spirit: Ripley's Believe It or Not! Museum.

The newest and grandest game in town is the $1.1 billion Borgata, which opened in 2003 in the marina district. Like the top Vegas casinos, the Borgata bypassed kitsch in favor of real luxury—dare we say *class?* With celebrity chefs like Bobby Flay and Wolfgang Puck and a superior spa, the Borgata leaves the coupon-clipping senior citizens to its competitors, going after the real money.

When casino gaming was approved in 1976, it was a lifeline for once-grand A.C., which had been hit hard by recession and

Atlantic City Casinos:

Since 1976, Shore casinos have provided the quickest way to make a buck—or lose your shirt.

changing tourist patterns. Long gone were the throngs of free-spending tourists who had pumped so much money into the Shore resort, leaving behind depressed neighborhoods, great pockets of deep poverty, and only memories of better times.

Though the casinos did bring jobs and hope to A.C., for years the glitz and glamour of the boardwalk casino hotels remained a bright façade that hid the miserable state of the many city blocks behind it. Eventually the Casino Redevelopment Association started delivering on its promises, funding many revitalization projects and building new homes in blighted areas.

Though far from problem-free, Atlantic City is now more vital and attractive than it has been for a very long time.

you know you're in
new jersey when...
... horsepower takes to the waves

Leave your kayak at home, but bring your ego and your wallet to the Atlantic City International Power Boat Show, or ACIPBS (www.acboatshow.com). One of the country's top exhibitions, it takes place every February in the A.C. Convention Center. With more than 700 boats on display in 500,000 square feet and a 90,000-square-foot Marine Marketplace, it's *the* place to contemplate some serious conspicuous consumption, with top price tags in the millions.

Well-known boating manufacturers like Bayliner, Chris Craft, and Viking bring their wares to Atlantic City. About 50,000 East Coast visitors show up to ogle motor and express yachts, sports fishermen, cruisers, and sport boats.

Boats showcased at the ACIPBS range in price from $5,000 to $1.7 million. Decked out with more bells and whistles than your average McMansion, the upscale yachts have it all—premium appliances, silverware, china, and cooking utensils in the galley; TV, satellite receiver, home theater, and wet bar in the salon; king-size bed and 5-foot tub in the master bedroom; and furnishings in fine Italian leather. In short, they are floating princely residences.

Even if you're in the "if you have to ask, you can't afford it" category, the show always has plenty to see. In 2006 one highlight was

"The Boats of Bond" exhibit, which included fantasy crafts from four decades of James Bond movies: the Tow Sled from *Thunderball* (1965); the Bath-o-Sub from *Diamonds Are Forever* (1971); the Glastron Amazon Chase boat from *Moonraker* (1979); the Neptune Submarine from *For Your Eyes Only* (1981); and the "Q" Jet Boat from *The World Is Not Enough* (1999).

If James Bond doesn't float your boat, the 2006 show also showcased the A.C. debut of Twiggy, the famous water-skiing squirrel.

Atlantic City International Power Boat Show:

At this annual event, you can be the captain of your own ship . . . for a price.

you know you're in
new jersey when...
... you don't need cement overshoes to sink to the bottom of the sea

Military engineers may come up with some bright ideas, but building ships out of concrete was not one of them. Back in World War I, when shipbuilding was hampered by a critical shortage of steel, the federal government dabbled with this experimental concept, planning an emergency fleet of 38 concrete ships. Due to various problems, only 12 were put into service; one was the *Atlantus,* whose name sounds curiously like that of a legendary island that sank to the bottom of the sea.

The *Atlantus* was the second prototype, a 3,000-ton, 250-foot-long freighter with a 5-inch-thick hull of special concrete aggregate. Built by the Liberty Shipbuilding Corporation of Brunswick, Georgia, the *Atlantus* was launched on November 21, 1918, at Wilmington, North Carolina, and commissioned on June 1, 1919. She served for a year as a government-owned, privately operated commercial coal steamer in New England.

When the war ended and the more efficient steel ships returned, the "Concrete Fleet" was decommissioned and the *Atlantus* was retired to Norfolk, Virginia. A year later the ship was purchased by a salvage company and stripped.

In 1926 the *Atlantus* was towed to Cape May to be used in the construction of a drawbridge, part of a new ferry project

Atlantus:

This sunken concrete ship has been lying off Cape May Point for more than 75 years.

from Cape May to Lewes, Delaware. But before she could be properly positioned, the *Atlantus* broke loose of her moorings during a storm and went aground.

Several futile attempts were made to free her, but all these years later, she still lies off Sunset Beach in Cape May Point. Thousands of visitors come each year to view remnants of the wreck (the bow is visible at low tide) and collect Cape May diamonds (see page 17), quartz crystals that grind down against its cracked, eroded hull and then wash ashore.

Contrary to popular belief, Abner Doubleday did not invent baseball in Cooperstown, NY; the first recorded organized baseball game was played on June 19, 1846, at Hoboken's Elysian Fields, later site of the Maxwell House Coffee plant. The rules were established by Alexander Cartwright, whose team, the Knickerbockers, played the New York Nine.

Soon the state had more than 150 teams for adults and youngsters. By 1900 baseball had truly become America's pastime, and practically every town in Jersey had a baseball team. Company teams like the Newark Westinghouse Nine, the Doherty Silk Sox of Paterson, and the Michelin Tire Company team of Millville were among the strongest.

New Jersey played particularly important roles in the beginning and the end of segregation in professional baseball. On July 4, 1887, at an exhibition game between the Newark Little Giants and the Chicago White Stockings, Chicago's Adrian "Cap" Anson refused to compete against the home team's black stars, pitcher George Stovey and catcher Fleetwood Walker. The eventual result was baseball's "gentleman's agreement" to exclude African Americans.

But Jersey already had the first documented black teams, the Cuban Giants of Trenton and the Long Branch Washingtons. Later the Atlantic City Bacharach Giants helped form the Eastern Colored League;

they won that pennant and brought the Negro League World Series to A.C. in 1926 and 1927.

The Depression hit the Negro Leagues hard, but they rebounded. The 1930s were a high point in Jersey baseball, with two great teams in Newark—the Negro League Eagles and the AAA Bears, owned by the powerhouse Yankees. Some consider the Bears the greatest minor league team ever.

When Jackie Robinson broke Major League Baseball's color barrier, the drain of talent and revenues killed the Negro Leagues. Fans remember Robinson as a Brooklyn Dodger, but his first game with a white team was at Roosevelt Stadium on April 18, 1946, when his Montreal Royals visited the Jersey City Giants.

Baseball:

American's pastime has been played on Garden State fields for more than 150 years.

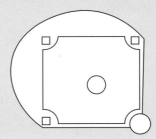

you know you're in
new jersey when...
...Smith is not just a name, it's a way of life

New Jersey played a major role in the success of the American Revolution, so it's not surprising that many reminders of that conflict are found here.

One of those reminders is Batsto Historic Village (www.batstovillage.org), located in magnificent Wharton State Forest in Hammonton. The village was founded in 1766 by Charles Read, the most noted ironmaster in west Jersey before the Revolution. It became the site of the Batsto Iron Works, which supplied Washington's Continental Army during the war.

Late in the 18th century, after the iron industry began to fail, William Richards bought the property and switched to the production of window glass. When the glass industry also declined almost a century later, Philadelphia financier/industrialist Joseph Wharton purchased the village and converted it into a gentleman's farm. He built a sawmill and an underground silo and enlarged the mansion. In 1954 the state of New Jersey bought Batsto, which is now listed on the National Register of Historic Places.

Today, the village's 33 historic buildings are like time capsules—scattered ironworkers' cottages, a sawmill, a modest general store filled with products your great-grandparents might remember, and a post office that still flies the 32-star American flag. (It's also one of only three post offices in the country where you can have your stamps hand-canceled.) Because of the site's historic significance, no zip code is required.

At the heart of the village is the mansion that was home to generations of ironmasters. When Wharton expanded it, he transformed the house into a grand, Italianate residence with 32 rooms, 14 of which are now open to the public. On weekends the resident potter and weaver might demonstrate their crafts, and when his schedule allows, the blacksmith fires up his forge and shows visitors the kind of work that was once so prevalent in this historic village.

Batsto:

This historic village and ironworks center supplied Washington's armies during the Revolutionary War.

Here in Jersey, we don't like to blow our own horn. But if there's one Jersey Girl that deserves a little more recognition, it's Big J, the battleship *New Jersey* (www.battleship newjersey.org).

The *New Jersey* is the nation's most decorated battleship, with 19 stars for battles and campaigns. She has seen more years of service and traveled more miles than any other U.S. Navy vessel. After sailing the seven seas, Big J is now enjoying a well-earned retirement in Camden, just a mile upriver from the Philadelphia Naval Shipyard, where she was built in 1940.

One of four Iowa-class battleships constructed during World War II (along with the *Missouri*, the *Wisconsin*, and the *Iowa*), the *New Jersey* measures 887 feet long and weighs in at 58,000 tons, with a beam of 108 feet. With the exception of two Japanese vessels, the Iowa-class battleships were the largest ever built and were capable of a maximum speed of 23 knots; their 16-inch guns could fire projectiles as far as 23 miles.

During World War II the *New Jersey* was active in the Pacific, participating in amphibious assaults on Iwo Jima and Okinawa. Big J was reactivated and used for shore bombardment in Korea and Vietnam; she played a similar role in Central America and off the coast of Lebanon before being decommissioned in 1991.

Battleship *New Jersey:*

The nation's most decorated ship, Big J has seen more service and traveled more miles than any other U.S. Navy vessel.

Opened to the public just weeks after September 11, 2001, Big J was greeted with waves of patriotic fervor; public officials pulled out their most stirring speeches, and former crew members wept. Today, you can tour the ship either on your own or with a docent. Guided tours around the upper and lower sections take about two hours. It's also possible to take a virtual tour in the ship's multimedia room.

...a world-famous Yogi enlightens you with his pearls of wisdom

Nowadays, everyone knows "It ain't over 'til it's over" and "You can observe a lot just by watching," but it took the inimitable Lawrence Peter Berra to point out these and other such truisms to us.

Although Berra was born in St. Louis, he has lived in Jersey for decades. According to one story, his wife asked where he would like to be buried: St. Louis; New York, where he played; or Montclair, his adopted hometown. The answer was classic Yogi: "Surprise me."

Montclair feels no such ambivalence. The town is home to the Yogi Berra Museum & Learning Center at Montclair State University (www.yogiberramuseum.org), a tribute to Berra's outstanding sports career. Kids who think that steroids and baseball are an inevitable coupling will see at the museum that it just ain't so.

Berra is the winningest player in World Series history, the true Mr. October. In his 17 full seasons with the powerhouse New York Yankees, he played in 14 World Series, alongside other Hall of Famers such as Joe DiMaggio, Mickey Mantle, Roger Maris, and Whitey Ford. The museum displays Berra's 10 championship rings, his vintage uniforms, and the mitt Berra used to catch Don Larsen's perfect game in the 1956 World Series against the crosstown rival Brooklyn Dodgers.

The museum's Canon Theater shows a film about Berra's life, as well as other baseball documentaries. Of course, if you're a fan from baseball's golden age, you might think, "It's déjà vu all over again," or worse, "The future ain't what it used to be."

You'll also find exhibits relating to the history of baseball—its pre-Civil War origins, how it became the national pastime in the late 19th century, and how integration later changed the game. Now, it goes without saying that the museum is open unless it's closed. Next door is Yogi Berra Stadium, home of the minor league New Jersey Jackals—so after a trip to the museum, you can take the kids out to the ball game.

Berra, Yogi:

This dugout philosopher may have been born in Missouri, but he's long called Jersey home.

you know you're in
new jersey when...
...you ride the rails in style

When the weather is balmy, there is no better way to explore the countryside in rural Hunterdon County than on the Black River and Western Railroad (www.brwrr.com), which runs for about 16 miles from Flemington to Ringoes.

This short-line railroad dates back to 1854, when the Flemington Transportation Company built the line from Flemington south to Lambertville, where it met the Pennsylvania Railroad. In those early days, dairy and fruit production in the area generated considerable rail traffic. Creameries along the line produced up to 6,000 gallons of milk a day, and two million trees produced much of the world's peach supply.

By 1885, 54 scheduled passenger trains entered and left Flemington each day. But over time traffic dwindled, and in April 1953 the last passenger train left the station. More than a decade later, the town of Flemington decided to run a tourist line on the still-operating freight rails. Governor Richard Hughes launched the project by cracking a bottle of champagne on the rear driver of Steam Locomotive #60 in May 1965.

The vintage passenger trains, a virtual museum on wheels, travel between the rural farmlands of Ringoes and historic Flemington on weekends and holidays from May through October; the ride costs $10

Black River and Western Railroad:

This 19th-century short-line railroad is now a tourist attraction and venue for private parties.

for adults. Special events run throughout the year, including the Easter Bunny Express, the Great Train Robbery, the Halloween Special, and the Santa Express. Black River also hosts birthday parties, private caboose charters, and wedding trains.

you know you're in
new jersey when...
...you pick your own antioxidants

Wild blueberries are indigenous to New Jersey. Native Americans used them in stews and in pemmican (dried venison), and to make natural blue dye. But it was a New Jersey farm woman who created the commercial highbush blueberry, first harvested in 1916.

Elizabeth White paid the local "Pineys," people who lived off the land in the isolated Pine Barrens, to mark the largest berry on each bush growing in the wild. Then "Miss Lizzie" and botanist Frederick Coville took thousands of cuttings, selecting the hardiest and most flavorful wild plants and crossing them with plants they already had. Many of the cultivated blueberries we see today are descendants of this original highbush variety.

White would be proud that New Jersey is the nation's second-largest producer (after Michigan) of blueberries. After all, she helped organize the New Jersey Blueberry Cooperative Association; she also was the first to put clear wrappers over small baskets of berries when they were shipped for sale.

The first Jersey blueberries are harvested in June, kicking off a celebration called the Red, White, and Blueberry Festival in downtown Hammonton, which bills itself the unofficial Blueberry Capital of the World. The event includes a stage show, an

Blueberries:

Whether you pick 'em at the farm or at your supermarket, blueberries are one of the healthiest things coming out of Jersey.

antique car show, food vendors, arts and crafts, lots of fresh-picked blueberries, all kinds of blueberry baked goods, and, of course, a blueberry pie-eating contest.

If pie-eating contests seem like just a spectacle of gluttony to you, keep in mind that blueberries are not only low in calories (only 42 per half cup) and high in fiber but also one of the most potent antioxidants, outscoring more than 40 other fruits and vegetables. So stick out your blue tongue and say, "Look, Ma, I've had my vitamins today!"

new jersey when...

... Boardwalk, Park Place, and Mediterranean are real places, not just Monopoly properties

Monopoly has familiarized budding young capitalists the world over with the streets and places of Atlantic City. Not for nothing are Boardwalk and Park Place the prime bits of real estate on the board: The intersection of these two "blues" marks the heart of the beachfront casino strip—the middle of it all.

Among its many tourism "firsts," Atlantic City claims the first boardwalk, built in 1870. It was the brainchild of Alexander Boardman, a conductor on the Camden and Atlantic Railroad, and Jacob Keim, an Atlantic City hotelier who hoped to reduce the amount of sand tracked into hotel lobbies and railroad parlor cars.

Built along the beachfront in 10-foot-wide portable sections, the first wooden footwalk was laid down by Memorial Day and picked up and stored after Labor Day. The new promenade was a huge success, and by 1897 A.C. was on its fifth boardwalk, which was up to 60 feet wide near the biggest hotels, as it is today.

At its most spectacular, Atlantic City's boardwalk stretched 10 miles—from Absecon Inlet to Longport. Spectacles, amusements, and refreshments of all sorts were offered on Young's Million Dollar Pier and the storied Steel Pier, where famous musicians from John Philip Sousa to Benny Goodman competed for tourist dollars with the famous high-diving horse.

Soon other Shore towns had their own boardwalks. Ritzy towns like Spring Lake and Sea Girt allowed no concessions, so their boardwalks provided a serene promenade. But anyone who has ever vacationed at the Shore remembers the amusements. Those once at Asbury Park and Long Branch are gone, but Seaside Heights still has its beach sky ride, a historic carousel, and a roller coaster hanging over the water.

With five amusement piers, 100 rides, and three water parks, Wildwood hosts the biggest amusement boardwalk in Jersey. Nearby Ocean City is a "dry" town, so its boardwalk is loaded with wholesome family fun—rides, waterslides, arcades, and all sorts of sticky candy to rot your teeth. In Keansburg the boardwalk is long gone, but the amusements remain.

Boardwalks:

Jersey boardwalks are beachfront promenades, some just for strolling, some busy with amusement arcades.

If Bruce is the workingman's poet, Jon Bon Jovi is the rock star *cum* heartthrob, riding his good looks and his big Jersey hair to fame and fortune with album sales of more than 100 million worldwide. Born John Francis Bongiovi in Perth Amboy, the rocker can thank his parents for his assets; his mother is a former Playboy bunny, and his father was the hairdresser who teased his son's coif to its 1980s heights.

John attended Sayreville War Memorial High School; he learned to play guitar and piano and got his first band together by age 13. After high school his uncle Tony got him a job as a janitor at the Power Station recording studio, where he was soon making demos with well-known musicians, including members of the E Street Band. One song, "Runaway," became a hit on local radio, so John formed a band to capitalize. In 1983 Polygram/Mercury signed the group and recast John's Italian name phonetically—and Bon Jovi was born.

"Runaway" became a Top 40 hit off Bon Jovi's 1984 debut album, and *7800 Fahrenheit* quickly went gold in 1985. International success followed with *Slippery When Wet*. That album featured the single "Wanted Dead or Alive," which made it to number seven on the *Billboard* charts and became the band's anthem.

No flash in the pan, Bon Jovi is still touring and recording, long after other '80s hair bands have broken up or gone bald. These days, the group's namesake devotes a good deal of his time and money to worthy nonprofit causes. Even more impressive, Jon is still married to his high school sweetheart, Dorothea, and they are raising their four children in Jersey (in a splendid riverfront château in the posh Navesink area of Middletown, quite a step up from Perth Amboy).

With his good looks, sexy voice, and a certain natural presence, Jon was made for the silver and small screens. He has appeared in at least eight feature films, and his TV credits include *Ally McBeal, Sex and the City,* and *The West Wing.* In the latter he pretty much played himself—a famous rock star stumping for Democratic candidates.

Bon Jovi, Jon:

His 2006 hit single, "Who Says You Can't Go Home?" says it all. This rocker lives with his family in Middletown.

14

you know you're in
new jersey when...
...you're on a first-name basis with The Boss

If you have to ask "Bruce who?" you are obviously not from Jersey. Even grandmas here know who The Boss is. Starting with his 1973 album *Greetings from Asbury Park*, Bruce forged a bond with his home-state audience, building a legend with marathon concerts lasting three or four hours.

His early songwriting style—ragged poetry loosely pegged to driving rock, with the guitar or sax waiting to bust loose—reached critical mass with the 1975 album *Born to Run*. From "Thunder Road" to "Jungleland," every song is an anthem, and when Bruce plays them in concert, thousands of voices chant back.

Of course they know the words. Many fans have been coming to The Boss's concerts for 20 years or more, and those lyrics recall their youth—warm summer nights, crummy locales from Asbury to Highway 9, recession, the betrayal and fraud of the American Dream, and the fast cars that promised to get you and your girl (Mary, Wendy, Cherry, Sherry Darling, and Rosalita) out of the trap. Some lines ring truer as listeners age:

So you're scared and you're thinking
That maybe we ain't that young anymore
Show a little faith, there's magic in the night
You ain't a beauty, but hey you're alright.

In 1984 Bruce had huge commercial success with *Born in the U.S.A.*, pure energy

Bruce:

Springsteen. But you knew that.

distilled into three- to four-minute radio-playable bites. The hits included "Glory Days" and "Bobby Jean" (which were a little more universal, a little less Jersey) and, of course, "My Hometown."

Also in 1984, Patti Scialfa joined the E Street Band, and seven years later the Jersey Girl married The Boss. Bruce and his family live in Rumson, with a place for horses in Colts Neck. Except for being a famous rock star, Bruce leads a fairly regular existence—you might see him at the video store, the market, or even the mall. In fact, when he's not on tour, Bruce thrills local crowds by showing up to jam with other rockers, especially at the Stone Pony in Asbury, where he and the E Street Band started out, and at local fundraisers like the Clearwater Festival.

you know you're in
new jersey when...
... your soup is M'm! M'm! Good!

Back in 1869 Joseph Campbell of Bridgeton and Abraham Anderson of Mount Holly went into the business of canning tomatoes. By 1897 their company had shifted focus and was canning condensed soups; among the first five varieties to bear the famous red-and-white label was Campbell's Tomato Soup.

For generations of Americans, Campbell has been a familiar part of everyday life. One devotee who immortalized his daily lunch routine was artist Andy Warhol, who took the can out of the closet and made it an icon of pop art with his screen-print series. Warhol was not alone in his soup selection, as Campbell remains the largest manufacturer of tomato soup in the world.

Everyone has his or her favorite—Chicken and Stars, Bean with Bacon, or Beef with Vegetables and Barley, which used to be so thick that it came out of the can in one solid piece. But the one creation that millions of Americans seem to agree on is Campbell's Cream of Mushroom soup, a key ingredient in green bean casserole. Although this dish is a must-have for Thanksgiving and other holiday dinners throughout the United States, few people realize that it originated in Jersey.

Created in the test kitchens of the Camden-based Campbell Soup Company back in 1955, green bean casserole has endured as

Campbell Soup Company:

Founded in Camden in 1869 by Joseph Campbell and Abraham Anderson, this successful business is now a household name.

a holiday tradition even as other 1950s-era back-of-the-package recipes have gone the way of the bomb shelter. Campbell estimates that it sells $20 million worth of Cream of Mushroom Soup every year just to satisfy the cravings of casserole aficionados.

True, many cooks have created their own variations on the casserole recipe over the years. But when the holiday season rolls around, more than 150,000 fans acquire the official recipe the modern way—by downloading it from www.campbell kitchen.com.

you know you're in
new jersey when...
... rumors of pirate treasure abound

Looking at Cape May today, it's hard to believe that this stately Victorian village was once the hub of pirate activity in south Jersey. Though most pirate tales involve accounts of buried treasure, some historians say that pirates had little treasure to bury, being given to drinking and carousing and generally living beyond their means. However, for those who are interested in tales of treasure, Jersey has plenty.

Captain Kidd, it is said, buried treasure somewhere around Ocean City before authorities caught him and took him back to England to be hanged. Captain Bartholomew Roberts supposedly lost a fortune in looted gold when one of his barques was sunk as he was attempting to run a blockade in Delaware Bay. And Blackbeard is said to have stashed some of his gold around Cape May, specifically on Higbee's Beach. Though gold coins occasionally wash ashore, we have never found any.

What visitors *can* find quite easily, on Sunset Beach in Cape May Point, are "Cape May diamonds," pure quartz crystals in a variety of colors. These stones originate in the upper reaches of the Delaware River, where they break off from larger quartz veins and pockets. They then travel some 200 miles via running water—a trip that takes as long as 1,000 years.

The "diamonds" are common on Sunset Beach because the strong tidal flow against the hulk of the sunken concrete ship *Atlantus* (see page 6) causes them to wash ashore. The largest Cape May diamond ever found weighed almost eight ounces.

When polished and faceted, the stones look just like real diamonds. They are popular souvenirs, sold in rings, earrings, and pendants in local shops. If you'd rather find your own "diamonds," you can buff them up and fool your friends into thinking you won the state lottery.

Cape May Diamonds:

These quartz crystals can be found on the beaches of Cape May County, from the Delaware Bay to Cape May Point.

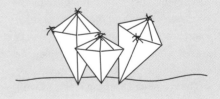

In spring, poets have said, a young man's fancy turns to love, and in Jersey, what men love are their wheels. The first warm days of spring coax open garage doors right along with the daffodils, and out pop the coddled trophy vehicles—the garishly colored muscle cars, the sleek sports cars, the convertibles.

Walk around almost any Jersey town in shirt-sleeve weather and you'll see men spending some quality time with their loved ones—chasing the dust off the white '72 'vette with the T-top, tuning up the orange '68 Road Runner with the black racing stripes on the hood, or easing that '64 Lincoln Continental with the suicide doors out of a standard-size garage with the tenderness and precision of a surgeon.

Where do you go once you've got those stylin' wheels rolling? Down the Shore, cars just seem to point east, to cruise by the boardwalk and taste the ocean breeze. Long Branch kicks off the summer season with the annual Cruise to the Jersey Shore (June). Musical nostalgia is always a big part of the warm-weather fun in this town; 1950s doo-wop bands usually give free open-air concerts during West End Cruise Night (July), while Big Band Swing Night (September) goes even further back in time.

Cruisin' to the Movies in Vineland (April) reunites vintage vehicles at a spot that

brings back memories for many teenagers now gone gray: the newly reclaimed Delsea Drive-in. Other shows focus on one particularly beloved model, like the Annual Mustang and Ford Fall Car Show in Mt. Laurel (September) or the Corvette Show in Smithville (October).

More casual are the monthly Kruise Nights in downtown Freehold (5:00 to 11:00 P.M. on the last Thursday of the month, from May through September).

But as Bruce explained in his tribute to American metallic excess, "Pink Cadillac," you don't even have to drive it—it's all about looking good.

Classic Cars:

For Jersey Guys, the metaphysical questions "Who are you?" and "Where are you going?" can be distilled into "What do you drive? How fast?"

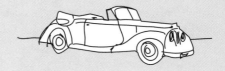

you know you're in
new jersey when...
...cowhands rope them dogies

Texas can go scratch our spurs because New Jersey lays claim to the longest-running Saturday-night rodeo in the United States, dating back to 1929.

Cowtown (www.cowtownrodeo.com), located between Woodstown and the Delaware Memorial Bridge, is not a cheesy theme park or a show. It's an honest-to-goodness rodeo with everything that western fans expect: good old-fashioned bareback bronco riding, steer wrestling, calf roping, team roping, Brahma bull-riding, and girls' barrel racing—all the stuff of classic cowboy movies, and then some.

From late May through September, the Saturday show begins at 7:30 P.M. and runs until about 10:00 P.M. But audience members are welcome to stay even later, as top-caliber contestants often perform after hours. (There are more contestants than performance time in the regular show.) No matter what the hour, no one goes hungry—warm peanuts, or goobers, are a staple at the rodeo.

If you have time to drive around before the show, you'll see miles and miles of open fields and fertile farmland, populated mostly by cattle and horses—a challenge to traditional notions of what New Jersey looks like. Horses and cattle raised here perform in rodeos all over the country, so if

Cowtown Rodeo:

Dating back to 1929, it's the longest-running Saturday-night rodeo in the United States.

you're a fan, you may already have seen one of these Cowtown animals.

Other events at Cowtown include a livestock auction and a flea market that promises "everything imaginable for sale" every Tuesday and Saturday.

Among the many new delicacies intro-duced to the Pilgrims by Native Americans were tart red berries called *Vaccinium macrocarpon*. Cranberries have been a Thanksgiving dinner staple ever since.

Unfortunately, the most familiar cranberry presentation is a can-shaped gel that over-worked holiday hosts put out as cranberry sauce. Fresh berries, available in the fall, have so much more to offer. And as the third-largest producer of cranberries in the United States, the Garden State knows how to grow this crop right. It thrives in the south Jersey Pinelands, where sandy, acid soil protects its roots from rotting.

Cranberries grow naturally along stream banks and in bogs. In the 1850s, farmer, inventor, and businessman J. J. White devised a method of cultivating cranberries in engineered bogs. Within 20 years he had established the farm known as Whitesbog and New Jersey as the country's leading producer of cranberries. (When disease decimated the cranberry harvest at the turn of the century, White's daughter Eliza-beth found a new cash crop: blueberries.)

Until the 1960s the berries were picked by a method known as dry harvesting, which is slow and laborious. Nowadays, when the crop is ready for harvest, the bogs are flooded and then churned by tractorlike machines, which allows the fruit to float to the surface and be more easily corralled.

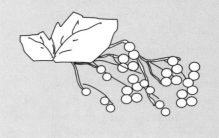

Cranberries:

Skip the can; buy this signature Jersey crop fresh in the fall.

Cranberry farming is a family affair. About 40 south Jersey families, some of them fifth-generation berry farmers, produce the state's crop these days. Once a precari-ously seasonal business, cranberry farming has become more stable thanks to cooper-atives, allowing a traditional way of life to thrive in the Pinelands.

Each year thousands of visitors travel to Chatsworth for the annual two-day Cran-berry Festival, which might include such entertainment as cranberry bog tours, the Antique and Classic Automobile Show, and/or a special appearance by the fabled Jersey Devil. The star of the festival is, of course, the cranberry in many permuta-tions: muffins, cake, preserves, salsa, and . . . well, you get the idea.

you know you're in
new jersey when...
... dead presidents aren't just in your wallet

OK, you caught us—neither Alexander Hamilton nor Aaron Burr was ever actually president, but they faced off in the most famous American duel outside of the O.K. Corral, on the bluffs of Weehawken. When it was over, one man was dead and the other was ruined.

Burr was born in Newark and graduated from the College of New Jersey (now Princeton). He was a commander in the Continental Army while still a teenager, leading attacks on the British at Hackensack and at the Battle of Monmouth. A Republican, Burr later became vice president under Thomas Jefferson.

Hamilton, who looks younger than ever on the new $10 bill, was the first secretary of the treasury under George Washington and signed the Constitution. A flamboyant Federalist who started the *New York Post*, Hamilton is sometimes called the "founder of Paterson" for spearheading the Society for the Establishment of Useful Manufactures (SUM), which proposed a $1 million investment in factories on the Passaic River.

Republicans were philosophically opposed to this sort of industrialization and helped scuttle the SUM as well as other Federalist projects, such as the development of the New Jersey side of the Hudson River, another Hamilton brainchild. These were just a few of the political turf battles that pitted Hamilton against Burr.

Whether his motives were political or personal, Hamilton detested Burr and didn't mind saying so publicly on at least one occasion. The insult reached Burr, and when Hamilton refused to apologize, Burr demanded satisfaction.

In the wee hours of July 11, 1804, Hamilton faced his challenger on a bluff overlooking the Hudson River. According to some accounts, Hamilton missed; others said he did not fire. Burr fired and hit Hamilton in the abdomen. Hamilton died the next day.

The actual rock "on which rested the head of Alexander Hamilton" after the duel is the base of the Death Rock monument, a bronze bust of Hamilton. Some years ago the rock was moved to Hamilton Avenue, a dead-end street in Weehawken.

Death Rock:

This artifact of the famous duel between Alexander Hamilton and Aaron Burr rests in Weehawken.

Deep Cut Gardens, like a number of places in Jersey, has a shady past. The original 35-acre scenic tract and the mansion that stood on it were bought in 1935 by Vito Genovese, the boss of the Genovese crime family.

Genovese wanted the grounds of his new home to remind him of his birthplace, Naples. He hired Theodore Stout to carry out his wishes, giving the designer a "spare no expense" mandate and a free hand. Well, almost a free hand. Though the house was in a Colonial revival style, Genovese wanted such Neapolitan touches as Italian statuary and a rock model of Mount Vesuvius.

To resolve a potential horticultural clash, Stout's final design incorporated a mixture of English- and Italian-style gardens, the latter with traditional terraced water pools. Below the house, the garden area was surrounded by a low stone wall and a masonry pergola, which still stands.

When Genovese was charged with murder in 1937, he fled to Italy and abandoned the property. Two weeks later the house burned down. These things happen in Jersey.

The property passed through several hands after that, eventually belonging to Karl and Marjorie Sperry Wihtol. In her will Marjorie donated half the property to the Monmouth County Park System, which pur-chased the remainder after her death in 1977.

The horticultural park opened to the public in 1978. It currently consists of 54 acres and offers commanding views of Atlantic Highlands and New York Harbor on clear days. Dedicated to the home gardener, the property is rich with exotic trees and shrubs. The gardens bring forth an abundance of daffodils in spring, a burst of tulips and magnolias in May, and a bounty of roses in summer.

Deep Cut Gardens:

Leave the stiletto at home—these flowers are just for looking.

you know you're in
new jersey when...
... Mr. Danny the hairdresser now takes a little off the top

"Five feet short" and virtually bald, Danny Michael DeVito is hardly your typical Hollywood leading man. Yet thanks to persistence and talent, he has made an extraordinary career as a character actor, often playing obnoxious or sinister types. DeVito also has achieved considerable success as a producer, with such films as *Erin Brockovich, Hoffa, Get Shorty,* and *Garden State.* His production company is called Jersey Films.

Born in Neptune on November 17, 1944, DeVito had a religious upbringing and attended Catholic schools. After graduating from Oratory Prep School in 1962, he took a job as a cosmetician at his sister's beauty shop. A year later, "Mr. Danny" enrolled in the American Academy of Dramatic Arts in New York to enhance his makeup skills— and instead was bitten by the acting bug. He made his screen debut in 1968 with a small part in *Dreams of Glass.*

Disappointments followed—he kept hearing "Nobody wants a 5-foot character actor"—so he decided to concentrate on the stage. During these early years of struggle, he met two people who would play an important part in his life: actor Michael Douglas, who would become a steady friend, and actress Rhea Perlman, who would become his wife.

DeVito, Danny:

This Neptune native is probably the only Hollywood producer who can do a French twist.

DeVito's first break came when he played Martini in the film version of *One Flew Over the Cuckoo's Nest,* reprising his stage role. DeVito didn't gain national recognition, however, until he was cast as Louie De Palma, the curmudgeonly dispatcher on the NBC sitcom *Taxi* (1978–83). DeVito later snagged major movie roles, including the Penguin in *Batman Returns,* a gambler in *Space Jam,* a sleazy agent in *Death to Smoochy,* and greedy businessmen in *Ruthless People* and *Other People's Money.*

DeVito's sister, Angela, still lives at the Shore, and DeVito has often been spotted in the Asbury Park area.

New Jersey is the diner capital of the United States, claiming about 570 such eateries (out of a nationwide total of approximately 3,000). About half of the state's towns have at least one diner. Drive down Route 130 from New Brunswick to Carneys Point and you'll pass almost two dozen.

The diner actually originated not in Jersey, but in Rhode Island. Back in 1872 Walter Scott started selling coffee and sandwiches from a horse-drawn wagon in Providence. Growing demand led to bigger, better facilities, and New Jersey companies responded—the Paterson Vehicle Company manufactured its first diner in 1928. Two of the three remaining diner manufacturers, Kullman and Paramount, are still based in Jersey.

Post–World War II car culture ushered in the golden age of diners, with the sleek stainless steel exteriors so typical of that era. Later, more elaborate façades became popular—Tudor, Mediterranean, and neo-classical styles all done in Garden State brickface. Interiors became flashier, with faux marble, gaudy fountains, and glass cases displaying towering cakes and pies.

But once the more traditional haunts started disappearing, nostalgia for the diners of old grew. Chains like Johnny Rockets and Checkers have tried to re-create the atmosphere of 1950s diners with retro furnishings and jukeboxes.

Diners:

Serving breakfast, lunch, and dinner at any hour of the day or night, Jersey diners are like a home away from home.

Moviemakers, too, now appreciate the diners' power to evoke a certain time and place. A number of Jersey diners have had their 15 minutes of fame: The Roadside Diner on Route 33 in Wall can be seen in *Baby, It's You* and in a Bon Jovi music video. The classic Bendix Diner on Route 17 in Hasbrouck Heights appeared in two movies, *Boys on the Side* and *Jersey Girl*. The Liberty View diner in Jersey City was in *Broadway Danny Rose*, while the Teamsters Diner in Fairfield was in *Angel Heart*.

Seen in commercials for Tums, the Harris Diner in East Orange is actually known for its fabulous breakfasts. The Little Ferry Diner, cast as Rosie's in the Bounty paper towel commercials, got so famous that it packed up and moved to Rockford, Michigan.

you know you're in
new jersey when...
...the summer sky glows with neon

Folks who live in Jersey or Philly know that *doo-wop* refers to a musical style made popular by groups like The Cadillacs and The Turbans. The term is also used to describe the unique architecture—also called *googie* or *populux*—that evolved from American pop culture of the 1950s and 1960s.

The town of Wildwood has some 220 buildings—the nation's largest concentration—in the doo-wop style. Back when Elvis was king and American cars sported big, flashy tail fins, Wildwood was a favorite family Shore resort, a neon-lit paradise of turquoise-and-white motels, noisy boardwalk amusements, and lively nightspots featuring stars like Frankie Avalon and Tony Bennett.

In most places, doo-wop architecture—with its tropical imagery and colors and space-age designs—faded and died. In Wildwood, thanks in part to the efforts of the Doo Wop Preservation League (www.doowopusa.org), googie is alive and thriving. There you'll find mom-and-pop motels painted in turquoise, orange, and pink, with Naugahyde, Formica, and chrome interiors. At Big Ernie's Fabulous '50s diner, the 1959 Seeburg jukebox plays vintage records for a dime.

In summer there are trolley tours of these flamboyant hot spots (starting at the Doo Wop Preservation League's headquarters). But even without a guide, it's easy to pick out such classic googie examples as the space-age Satellite, the swanky Starlux, and the exotic Tahiti motels.

At the Doo Wop Museum (3201 Pacific Avenue; www.doowopusa.org), you'll see vintage neon, Herman Miller chairs, Heywood Wakefield furniture, and items from designers Ray and Charles Eames. And if you do a club crawl at night during the summer season, you might even *hear* some authentic doo-wop to go along with the surroundings.

Doo-Wop Architecture:

You could call it "drive-in architecture"—it just goes with tail fins, poodle skirts, and early rock 'n' roll.

you know you're in
new jersey when...
...your weekend plans include going down the Shore

New Yorkers may spend weekends at the beach—that's the Hamptons or Fire Island. But if you're driving south on the Parkway on a Friday night, you're headed "down the Shore." After all, you can't go to the beach until you get to the Shore.

On Friday nights, weekenders join commuters and concertgoers on their way to the PNC Bank Arts Center in the congested southbound lanes. On Saturday morning, day-trippers with SUVs full of kids, summer-break college students meeting up with friends in Belmar or Manasquan, and gamblers bound for A.C. all try to get on the road before the traffic and heat build up. After all, it's no fun putting the top down if you're stuck bumper-to-bumper.

Some of the worst traffic is on exits and bridges to Point Pleasant. With its boardwalk amusements, weekly fireworks, great seafood restaurants, and busy marinas, there's a lot going on in a small space. Though attractions like Point Pleasant, Seaside Heights, and Wildwood may be among the best-known hot spots, the Jersey Shore has beaches to suit every mood.

Just south of Seaside Park but well-removed from the world of arcades and amusements is Island Beach State Park, a sublime slip of sand and dunes that stretches between ocean and bay. A different sort of back-to-nature crowd can be seen at Sandy Hook's Area E, the clothing-optional beach. If that sounds tantalizing, remember that it's not just bikini-ready babes who bare it all.

For the young and lithe, Belmar is one of the places to sun and be seen. Although baby oil and face reflectors have definitely gone out of style, you'll still see plenty of Jersey Girls who prep for the summer season at tanning salons. Less raucous than in the past, Belmar still has D'Jai's beachfront bar as well as pro sporting events like surfing and beach volleyball.

For party animals who prefer to limit their UV exposure, Sea Bright's many beachfront bars are like oases to the desert camel. Others may prefer to visit more exclusive towns like Deal or Spring Lake, where the sand is ritzier. For many families, private beach clubs like the Breakwater in Elberon and the Sea Watch in Manasquan are the place to reconnect with summer friends year after year.

Down the Shore:

In the words of The Boss, it's where "everything's alright, you and your baby on a Saturday night."

Given our state's love affair with cars, it's no surprise that New Jersey had the first drive-in theater, invented by Richard M. Hollingshead Jr. of Camden in 1933.

Hollingshead observed that moviegoing was not a family activity: Kids went to matinees; adults went to evening showings. The adult outings entailed finding a babysitter and looking for parking. Hollingshead's brainstorm let parents get out of the house and bring the kids along.

Hollingshead tested his idea in his backyard, mounting a 1928 Kodak projector on the hood of his car and nailing a screen to a couple of trees. With a radio playing behind the screen, he rolled the windows to various positions to test for optimum sound. To simulate rain, he turned on his sprinklers. To test sightlines, he lined up cars in his driveway at different angles.

With three investors behind him, Hollingshead took out patent number 1,909,537 for the first drive-in theater in May 1933. Three weeks and $30,000 later, the simply named Drive-In Theatre opened on Crescent Boulevard in Camden. Admission was 25 cents per car and 25 cents for each person in the car, with a maximum admission of $1.00—offering the ultimate in affordable family entertainment.

The drive-in became an instant success, not just with families but with young couples

Drive-ins:

With this invention, Richard M. Hollingshead Jr. of Camden made moviegoing a family affair.

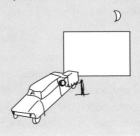

who could find privacy in cars—hence the fond nickname "passion pits." Drive-ins reached their peak in the car-loving 1950s; the state counted 44 such theaters in 1958.

Many passersby recall the Perth Amboy drive-in, whose huge screen was all too visible from the Garden State Parkway and Routes 1 and 9. The R-rated features shown there were known to distract drivers and cause the occasional fender-bender.

Economics eventually spelled the end for Jersey's drive-ins; theaters make more money selling individual tickets as well as snacks. But now, thanks to John and Judith DeLeonardis, who have revived the Delsea Drive-In in Vineland, Jerseyans can once again go to the movies with their kids, pillows, and pajamas.

The story of Doris Duke's failed marriages, her isolated final years, and her lonely death in 1993 seem to prove the old adage that "money can't buy happiness." But as a younger woman, the billionaire tobacco heiress lived a life that—at least on the surface—was the stuff of fairy tales.

One of her several homes was the Somerville estate she inherited from her father, James Buchanan Duke. James had bought the land in 1893 and spent, according to some accounts, about $10 million to create roadways, hills, lakes, and fountains. For his personal Eden, he imported shrubs and trees from all over the world.

After his death Doris took over the estate, which required a staff of about 400 to maintain. She added an indoor skeet-shooting range and an 18-hole golf course and developed exotic display gardens in her father's honor, using Pennsylvania's Longwood Gardens as inspiration. For the next 20 years, 15 full-time employees worked on the gardens.

In 1964 the heiress opened an acre of land on her 2,700-acre estate for public visitation. After her death and in accordance with her wishes, the gardens were opened to visitors (www.dukefarms.org).

Even to jaded eyes, Duke Gardens is a magical place, with displays inspired by coun-

Duke Gardens:

These magnificent gardens were created by tobacco heiress Doris Duke on her estate in Somerville.

tries in all corners of the globe. There are English, Chinese, Japanese, French, Indo-Persian, Colonial, Edwardian, American Desert, and Tropical Jungle styles. Doris was an expert on orchids, and the Edwardian garden is filled with these gorgeous blooms, most of them in the mauve color that was popular with wealthy Americans in the late 19th century.

The doors of Country Manor—Duke's 67,000-square-foot, 55-room private residence—opened in July 2005. Public tours are being offered for a limited period while the Doris Duke Charitable Foundation contemplates future use of the mansion.

you know you're in
new jersey when...
... you get a really bright idea

The story of Thomas Alva Edison is an object lesson to those who think that any kid who can't conform has A.D.D. Young Tom was always curious, asking questions about how things worked. This worried some of his teachers (possibly because they had no answers), so they considered him retarded. After only three months in the classroom, Edison left school to be taught by his mother.

At age 12 he was selling newspapers on the railroad, where he also conducted chemistry experiments and learned how to operate a telegraph. His first patented invention, in 1868, was an electric vote-recording machine. Legislatures weren't interested (hmmmm), so he focused on saleable devices such as an improved stock ticker. He then opened a laboratory in Newark and made improvements in telegraphy and on the typewriter.

In 1876 Edison built a laboratory in Menlo Park, where he gave life to some of his greatest inventions. The cylinder phonograph, the first sound recording device ever, made him a celebrity. It was there, too, that Edison gave the world the electric light—he not only invented the incandescent lightbulb but also developed a complete system for supplying electric power to homes.

In 1887 Edison moved to a larger laboratory in West Orange, where he worked on motion pictures. Though he was a fairly shrewd businessman, he failed to realize profits in this business. During World War I he researched such devices as the submarine periscope and torpedo mechanisms for the U.S. military.

When he died in 1931, Edison held more than 1,000 patents. Among his inventions were the storage battery, the dictaphone, and the mimeograph machine. He also invented or worked on many of the modern conveniences we take for granted today.

In 1937 the 130-foot-tall Thomas Alva Edison Memorial Tower was built to mark the spot where the lightbulb was invented. Next door, the Menlo Park Museum (www.menloparkmuseum.com) houses products from the Thomas A. Edison Co., photographs of Edison's laboratory, and the inventor's death mask, made in 1931 by noted American sculptor James Earl Fraser.

Edison, Thomas Alva:

The Wizard of Menlo Park was one of the greatest inventors of the modern era.

Just a lot of smelly highway between the City and A.C. or Philly—that's what most New Yorkers think of Jersey. The nastiest part is right around exit 13A on the Turnpike, the heart of Jersey's industrial corridor. There, the otherworldly Linden Cogeneration Plant hisses smoke; it looks even spookier lit up at night.

Afterburners dot the area like beacons, but in February 2003 these flames of industry reached epic proportions when one of Hess Oil's storage tanks caught fire. The smoke and flames reached hundreds of feet in the air and could be seen for miles.

It's no surprise that New Jersey has the most Superfund hazardous waste sites of any state (113 as of April 2005, according to one state document). The nation's most densely populated state, New Jersey was also one of its first centers for heavy industry, with numerous chemical, petrochemical, pharmaceutical, and manufacturing installations. These plants were built decades before the U.S. government regulated dumping or Canada started whining about acid rain.

Factories (and gangsters) in New York and Philly found that the cheapest way to dispose of anything was to drive it to a lonely spot in Jersey. No wonder we're fed up with taking garbage from New York. But New Jersey also leads the country in contaminated sites that have been cleaned up—16 since 1986.

The ocean is cleaner, too. When used syringes started coming in with the tide, the Clean Ocean Action Committee mobilized volunteers to do beach cleanups. They collected the medical waste and were able to pinpoint the source—New York City hospitals illegally dumping biohazards at sea.

Now land in Jersey has gotten too valuable to waste. A disused gravel quarry about 20 minutes from Philadelphia is now a challenging golf course, Scotland Run. And Bayonne Golf Club, built atop the old city dump, is an almost surreal experience. From its fescue-covered dunes, spectacular views take in Manhattan skyscrapers and chemical storage tanks, container shipping and sailing yachts. Memberships are the hottest commodity on Wall Street.

Flames of Industry:

Our state motto could be "The *New* New Jersey—Now with 10 Percent Less Toxic Waste!" It's actually true.

new jersey when...

... you park in the driveway and drive on the Parkway

Perhaps no other state is as closely identified with its highways as Jersey. In the opening credits of *The Sopranos,* flashes of driving on the New Jersey Turnpike situate the viewer squarely in the Garden State. The 148-mile-long thoroughfare, which traverses the state from the Delaware Memorial Bridge in the southwestern corner to the George Washington Bridge in the northeast, is the nation's busiest limited-access nonstop toll road.

For many of us, the Garden State Parkway, which runs from the New York state border to Cape May, is the road to the Shore. The interchange from the much grittier Turnpike to the scenic, wooded Parkway used to make you feel like you were getting closer to the country (less so now that townhouse developments are encroaching on every side).

Built in the 1950s, the Parkway was innovative in its accommodations for high-speed traffic. It featured access via long acceleration ramps; no intersections; and a wide, wooded center median to reduce glare from oncoming traffic. The New Jersey Highway Authority (NJHA), which oversees the Parkway, even takes credit for the invention of rumble strips to wake up drifting drivers.

If you live in a small town in Jersey and you try to explain where it is, you will inevitably

Garden State Parkway and New Jersey Turnpike:

These two toll roads will take you anywhere in Jersey—for a price.

be asked, "What exit?" Sometimes the question is posed in a genuine effort to pinpoint your locale, and sometimes it's a feeble put-down from out-of-staters. Of course, if you're from Jersey, you'll have no trouble telling the difference and responding appropriately.

Incidentally, both highways are toll roads. This pernicious form of highway robbery dates back to the early 1700s, when what is now Norwood Avenue was part of the Long Branch–Deal Turnpike; fees were collected at the corner of Roseld Avenue, presumably to improve roads throughout Monmouth County.

Smug New Yorkers like to think they're savvier than the "bridge and tunnel crowd," but one place where they've been sold a bill of goods is at the gas pump.

Outside the Garden State's hourglass-shape borders and bubble of protection, any driver who needs to refuel is obliged to descend from the climate-controlled comfort of his vehicle, roll up his sleeves, and work the pump himself—that is, unless he cares to pay a premium of 20 or 30 cents per gallon over and above already outrageous gas prices.

Whether it's raining or snowing, blazing sun or dark of night, in 48 of the 50 United States drivers are obliged to dialogue with the computerized gas pump or scurry into the station's convenience store, where the attendant lazes behind his cash register. Then, they must pop off the gas cap and inhale *eau de petroleum* while fumbling with the unwieldy pump, all the while guarding their Armani suits and Gucci pumps (gasoline doesn't do much for wool or fine leather).

Not in New Jersey, where such activity is not only unnecessary but also illegal. Industry flacks tell us that self-service gas is increasingly popular in the United States. It's certainly popular with the companies that sell gas, as they can man *non*-service stations more cheaply and get the con-

Gas:

Jersey is one of only two states that prohibit self-serve gas—and we like it that way.

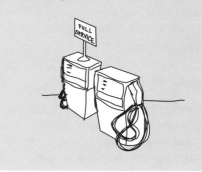

sumer into the retail shop to buy soda and candy.

Lobbyists have been trying, so far unsuccessfully, to convince lawmakers in Jersey and Oregon (the other civilized state that prohibits self-serve) to switch. Recent reports from Oregon indicate that there's not a chance that they'll agree. We salute them and urge them to hang tough. Save the jobs of some 7,600 professional gas station attendants and the wardrobes of an entire state.

you know you're in
new jersey when...

...you don't have to be Humpty Dumpty to have a great fall

Also known as the Passaic Falls, Paterson's Great Falls tumbles down a 77-foot-tall cataract in the Passaic River's path to the sea. It is the second largest waterfall east of the Mississippi, runner-up only to that largish falls in western New York.

The state's most impressive natural wonder was not destined to remain unspoiled. When he was secretary of the treasury, Alexander Hamilton envisioned Totowa Falls, as it was then called, as a source of power for a new national manufacturing complex to be run by the Society for the Establishment of Useful Manufactures (SUM). The mismanaged SUM was a political and financial disaster until the War of 1812 cut off imports from England.

Paterson manufacturing then took off, especially silk and textile garment production. These industries provided many new immigrants with jobs until the end of the 20th century, when most textile production moved overseas. Also produced in Paterson during that period were steam locomotives, textile machinery, revolvers, and aircraft engines.

In 1945 the SUM sold all its assets and rights to the City of Paterson. In 1971 the nonprofit Great Falls Preservation and Development Corporation was established to restore and redevelop the historic mill buildings and raceways. On June 6, 1976,

President Gerald Ford visited Paterson and designated the Great Falls/SUM district a National Historic Landmark. It is now called Great Falls State Park.

With bridges straddling the river and great, disused brick factories surrounding it, the Great Falls of the Passaic River is less than pristine. The river is certainly cleaner than it's been in a long time, though, largely because much of the manufacturing base has deserted this gritty city.

The City of Paterson's Great Falls Visitor Center (973–279–9587), located across from the Great Falls at 65 McBride Avenue Extension, offers guided walks and a historic interpretation of the district.

Great Falls:

A 77-foot-tall cataract is the focal point of Great Falls State Park, once a manufacturing center and now a National Historic Landmark.

In the summer of 1858, fossil hobbyist William Parker Foulke was vacationing in Haddonfield when he learned of an earlier find at a local marl pit. (Marl is a mixture of marine clay or shale.) Workers had unearthed giant bones that no one could identify.

Intrigued and excited, Foulke hired a crew and spent the rest of the summer and fall shin-deep in gray slime. What emerged from the pits were the fossilized remains of a Cretaceous-era animal larger than an elephant, with the structural features of both a lizard and a bird. It was named *Hadrosaurus foulkii,* which means "Foulke's large lizard."

Foulke had uncovered the first nearly complete skeleton of a dinosaur, a find that would change prevailing notions about dinosaurs. Foulke's partner, Joseph Leidy, concluded that Hadrosaurus could walk upright, given its relatively short upper arm bone. The skeleton created a sensation at Philadelphia's Academy of Natural Sciences in 1868, when it became the first dinosaur ever on public display.

The duck-billed Hadrosaurus was designated New Jersey's official state dinosaur in 1991, although the state's abundant Cretaceous deposits have yielded a number of other fossils: Dryptosaurus, Nodosaurus, and Coelurus.

The historic site of Foulke's discovery in Haddonfield includes a modest marker, a commemorative stone, and a tiny park. Just beyond the stone, the ground drops away into the steep ravine where the bones of *Hadrosaurus foulkii* were originally excavated. Visitors can climb down into the 30-foot chasm to stand at the actual marl pit where Foulke made his momentous discovery.

For many locals, Howell sculptor Jim Gary brought the age of dinosaurs into the present when he built whimsically colored dinosaurs out of old car parts. His towering creations have been exhibited in museums worldwide, including Jersey's Liberty Science Center. Before his death in 2006, Gary often had a dozen or more of his mammoth constructions in his backyard, gaily lit during the Christmas season.

Hadrosaurus:

This official state dinosaur was discovered in Haddonfield in 1858.

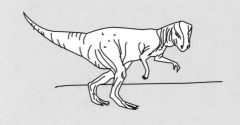

new jersey when...

...the age of dirigibles goes up in flames

On May 6, 1937, the German dirigible LZ-129 *Hindenburg* exploded into flames in the skies over Naval Air Station Lakehurst in Ocean County. Nicknamed the "Titanic of the Sky" in a documentary of that name, the *Hindenburg* has become synonymous with disasters of epic proportions.

At 803.8 feet in length and 135.1 feet in diameter, the German passenger airship was a veritable flying luxury hotel, the largest aircraft ever to fly. The commercial flights of the *Hindenburg,* along with the *Graf Zeppelin,* pioneered the first transatlantic air service. The *Hindenburg* carried hundreds of passengers and traveled thousands of miles before its ill-fated flight to New Jersey.

Lakehurst was the center for Lighter-than-Air (LTA) aeronautics in the United States. The first blimp that came to Lakehurst was the *Shenandoah*; it arrived in 1924 and perished in turbulence a year later. Other tragedies shook the public's confidence in LTA. Then came bigger and better airships such as the *Graf Zeppelin,* which logged more than a million miles, including a round-the-world flight that began and ended at Lakehurst.

But on that day in May when the *Hindenburg* exploded in midair, killing more than 30 people (most died after jumping from the aircraft), rigid-airship development also

Hindenburg Disaster:

Thirty-six people died when a German dirigible exploded over Naval Air Station Lakehurst in eastern New Jersey.

died. Today, the Navy Lakehurst Historical Society museum (www.nlhs.com) preserves 40 years of aeronautical history with exhibits such as a replica of the *Hindenburg* gondola. Free tours of the crash site, the memorials, the blimp hangars, and other artifacts are given the second Saturday of each month.

you know you're in
new jersey when...

... the state slogan could be "It's Jersey: Got a Problem with That?"

When state officials decided that the old advertising slogan "NJ and You: Perfect Together" was dated, they paid Lippincott Mercer, a New York image consultant firm, $260,000 to come up with a new one.

The best the firm could offer was "New Jersey: We'll Win You Over." Needless to say, residents were disgusted with both the motto and the fee paid to this out-of-state company. Even acting governor Richard Codey thought it sounded pathetic, like some loser begging for a date.

Sure that citizens of the state could do better, Codey opened the debate to the public. Great suggestions came in a variety of tones, from exuberant ("New Jersey: The Beach, The Boss, The Best") to slightly defensive ("New Jersey: Laugh It Up, We Got More Money than *Your* State") to cryptic ("Yo Joisey: Politicos and Wiseguys, Bada-bing!").

Some politicized slogans made good points: "New Jersey: Most of Our Elected Officials Have Not Been Indicted" and "New Jersey: We Had a Gay Governor, So What?" Despite all of these great submissions, the winner chosen by Internet poll was "New Jersey: Come See for Yourself."

Regardless of the outcome, the contest showcased what we call Jersey Attitude. It's a little like pornography: difficult to define, but you know it when you see it—or hear it.

Every episode of *The Sopranos* is rich with it: the edgy speech, the body language that says "Don't p— me off."

But it's not just about gangsters and hoodlums. We are awed by British actor Hugh Laurie, who plays the genius doctor on Fox Network's *House,* set in the Princeton area. Laurie perfectly captures the character's Jersey Attitude, which translates to "Ignore my advice, and you'll die."

How do you know if you've got Jersey Attitude? Try this simple test: When someone says "Have a nice day," you

- A) respond "Thanks, you too."
- B) say nothing but are vaguely irritated.
- C) reply "Bite me," accompanied by a hand gesture.

Do you really need the answer?

Jersey Attitude:

Mix one part gallows humor and two parts sarcasm to get 100% pure Jersey Attitude.

you know you're in
new jersey when...
... eastbound is eastbound and westbound is westbound, and never the twain shall meet

With 34,268 miles of highway, New Jersey is the country's most highway-dense state. This is even more impressive when you consider that the vast Pine Barrens in the south are virtually undeveloped.

The abundant highway system obviously has not escaped the notice of insurance carriers, who saddle New Jerseyans with some of the highest auto insurance premiums in the country. Accident statistics seem to prove that New Jerseyans are not as skilled drivers as, say, Kansans. But those straight-highway drivers would fall apart if they had to deal with the situations we see every day, including high-speed traffic hemmed in by Jersey barriers.

On the wide-open plains, 40 or 50 feet can be spared for a median. Other states use low steel guardrails to flank traffic, but these are costly—not to mention dangerous to repair, especially in the midst of high-volume, two-way traffic. Furthermore, a metal barrier will not necessarily stop an 18-wheeler from plowing into oncoming cars.

The dangers were especially high in populous areas like Hudson and Essex Counties. So more than 50 years ago, the New Jersey State Highway Department devised the Jersey barrier, a tapered concrete wall. Its shape turns an impacting vehicle's momentum upward, which prevents the vehicle from rolling over.

Jersey Barriers:

Also called Jersey dividers, these concrete structures are a common sight on state highways.

To be sure, these concrete colossi can be intimidating, especially in construction zones, where they narrow lanes to the barest minimum. But to Jersey drivers they're just one more hazard to contend with every day—like jughandles, traffic circles, outrageous toll roads, and Bennies (i.e., New Yorkers) who can't drive and have no idea where they're going.

Sports fans may think that Jersey's National Hockey League team was named the Devils just to intimidate the competition. But natives know that the moniker comes from the state's legendary monster.

Stories about the Jersey Devil vary, but the most common date back to a dark and stormy night (is there any other kind of night for weird happenings?) in 1735, when a Mrs. Leeds was giving birth to her 13th child. During her labor, she cursed the baby, saying: "Let this child be born a devil!"

A beautiful boy was born, but to the horror of both mother and midwife, the boy began to mutate. His face elongated, as did his legs; his feet became hoofs. Dark wings sprouted from his shoulders—and then the creature let out a piercing scream and flew out into the night.

Since then the Devil has been sighted regularly in and around the Pine Barrens, in other Jersey towns, and even as far away as New York. Altogether there have been about 2,000 sightings, often by sober and respectable citizens. Supposedly there was even an exorcism by a cleric; that ritual was said to have put the creature to sleep for a century.

In the 19th century, Commodore Stephen Decatur claimed that he shot the creature,

Jersey Devil:

Thousands of (mostly) sober and respectable citizens have claimed to see this legendary monster.

which kept on flying. Joseph Bonaparte, a former king of Spain and brother of Napoleon, said that he spotted the Devil in Bordentown. In 1909 the appearances increased dramatically, with more than 1,000 sightings that year.

According to superstition, the Devil appears as a portent before disasters. He was reportedly seen before the start of the Civil War, the Spanish-American War, both World Wars, and the Vietnam conflict. Some witnesses claim to have seen him on December 7, 1941, just before Pearl Harbor was bombed. Believers say that it's the Devil's demonic origins that make him a harbinger of disaster.

you know you're in
new jersey when...
...big hair never goes out of style

Take it from The Boss: When you're in love with a Jersey Girl, "everything's gonna be alright." He should know. His first marriage to Oregonian Julianne Phillips was an also-ran, but his union with Patty Scialfa—"the First Lady of Love," as he calls her onstage, and a native of Deal—has been going strong since 1991.

Being Jersey isn't just about where you were born. Fans of *The Sopranos* might immediately peg Edie Falco and Drea de Matteo (Carmela and Adriana) as arche-typal Jersey Girls. Though Falco was born in Brooklyn and de Matteo in Queens, they get honorary status for playing their parts to a T. Conversely, Meryl Streep hails from posh Bernardsville, but you'd hardly think of the Oscar winner as a Jersey Girl.

It's all about hair, heels, and attitude.

A real Jersey Girl is not a shrinking violet. She's got a no-nonsense, don't-jerk-my-chain demeanor. Not that Jersey Girls don't fall for gold-wearing, Corvette-driving Jersey Guys with a line of B.S. from here to Atlantic City, because they do. That mating ritual takes place on Saturday night at clubs like Bar A in Belmar and Jenkinson's in Point Pleasant, where teasing is not just a hair-grooming technique, it's a way of life.

Speaking of teasing, fashion mags periodically pronounce that big hair is "out" or it's "back"; they hardly slow the sales of super-stiff hair gels and sprays in the Garden State. Back in the 1960s, at beauty salons with names like Mr. Carmine's, you could get a 'do that would barely fit into your car. In the *Flashdance*-era 1980s, Jersey Girls applied the techniques of back-combing and spraying to layered haircuts, creating volume of unheard-of proportions. Today, up-and-coming Jersey Girls start young, dabbling in highlights at the tenderest of ages.

When it comes to footwear, a real Jersey Girl can drive a stick in 6-inch Jimmy Choos. But a taste for stilettos doesn't mean she's a pushover or an airhead. Think of actress Bitty Schram of Mountainside. On the television show *Monk,* her character (Sharona Fleming) chased criminals and kept her neurotic employer in line without relinquishing her high-heel boots.

Jersey Girls:

Are different from New York girls.

new jersey when...

...it's last names only

If you're from Jersey, you probably think that the title of this book really should have omitted the word *New,* as most of us do in everyday speech. We tried, but were overruled.

Other states proudly go by their nicknames, but call New Jersey the Garden State, and people will snicker. We stick with just plain *Jersey,* as in, "I didn't know he was from Jersey," or "Call me when you get back to Jersey." These sentences don't work at all with other states beginning with *New.*

Certain areas have their own bits of Jersey-speak. Jersey Shore natives call summer people from Up North (anywhere beyond New Brunswick) "Bennies" and blame them for problems like traffic, litter, and inflated real estate prices. You hear this less and less, now that transplanted Bennies are in the majority.

Folks in rural southern Jersey are "Pineys," a reference to the Pine Barrens. Parts of Salem and Cumberland Counties on the Delaware Bay, sometimes identified as "Down Jersey," are so rural that residents are proud to be called Pineys.

Now we come to the "deeze" and "doze" expressions familiar to fans of *The Sopranos* and commonly considered part of the Joisey accent. *Fuhgeddaboutit!* according to William Labov, co-author of the *Atlas of North American English,* an encyclopedia of regional accents. Like much of our haz-ardous waste problem, the accent is a New York import.

Mr. Labov, a Rutherford native, informed *The New York Times* that there is no such thing as a Jersey accent: "What we have in Jersey is a continuum of two patterns. In North Jersey . . . it makes no difference whether you're talking about the New York City pattern or the New Jersey pattern, because they're going to be similar. And Jersey definitely is not the tail wagging the New York City dog."

Labov added, "Once you get to South Jersey, you're well into the Philadelphia system, an entirely different nasal system." Down south, they swallow their *ells* right along with their cheesesteak.

Jersey-Speak:

Residents have their own way of saying things—starting with the state name, which is one word too long for most natives.

Everyone in Jersey looks forward to summer—not just for the long, lazy days at the beach, but for the Jersey produce that appears at local farm stands and vegetable markets. Jersey tomatoes are a particular favorite. So juicy and flavorful, they are delicious with just a sprinkle of salt or, better yet, in a simple *Caprese* salad, with fresh mozzarella and basil leaves dressed with salt, pepper, and olive oil.

Supermarket tomatoes from California and Mexico are thick-skinned varieties that can withstand mechanical harvesting. They are picked green, refrigerated, and then gassed with ethylene to make them turn red during shipping. Yuk! Savvy shoppers have come to recognize that those dubious pale orange orbs in their cellophane boxes of three are tomatoes in name only; inside they're usually dry, mealy, and tasteless.

Jersey tomatoes are vine-ripened and picked just a few days before complete maturity, when the fruit is well developed and the seed cavity has a jellylike consistency. (If pickers waited until the tomatoes were completely red, the produce would be soft and easily crushed during shipment.) To guarantee that "Jersey Fresh" taste, farmers make frequent deliveries of smaller quantities of tomatoes to local supermarkets. Extended storage and/or transportation just aren't acceptable.

Jersey Tomatoes:

Vine-ripened Jerseys are juicy and delicious, the flavor of summer.

To get the most out of your Jerseys, choose tomatoes that are small enough to finish at one meal; one study showed that a sliced tomato begins to lose flavor three minutes after it is cut.

Do not refrigerate Jersey tomatoes; it destroys their natural taste. Store them at room temperature (not above 78 degrees Fahrenheit) in a cool, dark place—not on a windowsill, as light actually curtails the ripening process. Tomatoes are ready to eat when they are slightly soft to the touch but not mushy.

A bit of local etiquette: When arriving at a cookout, there's no better hostess gift than tomatoes from your own backyard or a bag of fresh Jersey corn. We could go on and on about Jersey corn, too, but we had to leave 'em something to write about in *You Know You're in Iowa When . . .*

you know you're in
new jersey when...

...your latest hobby is making jughandles

If you were to go by the number of times you're likely to hear the phrase "make a jughandle," you might think that the entire state of New Jersey is populated by amateur potters. Not so (although there are more and more of these kiln-for-hire places cropping up).

If you're from out of state, you may be confronted with the phrase under trying circumstances, namely when you make a wrong turn and stop to ask for directions. The reply could go something like this: "Turn around and go back the way you came about half a mile. When your get to the highway, go through the traffic light and make the jughandle, and then you'll be heading south again."

Now, if you're leery about encountering Jersey Attitude (see page 36), you might just nod and say "thanks" without actually having a clue as to what you're supposed to do. Fortunately, we're here to explain it.

A jughandle is the Jersey way of making a left turn without creating gridlock or getting broadsided at high speed. At many, if not most, highway intersections there is a sign (or several signs) prominently proclaiming NO LEFT TURN. As you gaze wistfully in your intended direction of travel, control your emotions and resist the temptation to defy the sign. Jersey traffic cops are pretty

Jughandle:

This term refers to the roundabout Jersey way of making a left or U-turn.

vigilant, but not half as expressive as the line of traffic you're holding up.

Instead, quickly move into the right-hand lane. Proceed through the intersection, make a looping, 270-degree right turn, and *voilà,* you're on course.

Welcome to Jersey driving. You've already learned how to navigate our highways and stay in your car while gassing up (see pages 37 and 32, respectively). Next lesson: traffic circles.

you know you're in
new jersey when...
... amusement parks are the way they used to be

"Old-fashioned" is a term of endearment when applied to a century-old amusement park that evokes memories of childhood. Keansburg is a nice combination of the classics that we begged Mom to let us ride and the high-tech stuff our kids now beg us to let them ride.

There's something for every member of the family to enjoy. Nostalgia fans will gravitate to the beautiful carousel, the bumper cars, and the Ferris wheel. Younger visitors may assess the scream potential of newer rides, such as the Moby Dick (a rotating platform), while the more daring may be attracted to high-tech thrills like the Double Shot and Pharaoh's Fury.

There are some 40 rides in all, including many suitable for younger children (among them a kiddie coaster called the Sea Serpent and the ever-popular go-karts), as well arcades, games of chance, and food concessions. The prices are a bit gentler than those at glitzy, newfangled parks. Other attractions at Keansburg include a 2,500-foot fishing pier and a free bayshore beach.

There have been some changes and additions over the years. The Gehlhaus brothers, grandsons of the park's founder, completed a multimillion-dollar rehab that included the Runaway Rapids Waterpark, which has tropical landscaping and a dozen thrilling slides. If it's speed or excitement

you want, try the toboggan-style slide or the wet-and-wild obstacle course. For a more relaxing afternoon, go with the lazy river or lounge in the spa pool.

For hours of operation and more information on attractions, visit the Keansburg Amusement Park Web site at www.keansburg amusementpark.com.

Keansburg Amusement Park:

This family-friendly park features classic rides and old-fashioned fun.

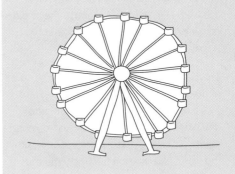

43

you know you're in
new jersey when...
...applejack is no kid's cereal

Trix may be for kids, but New Jersey apple-jack may have you seeing tricky rabbits.

Called "Jersey Lightning," applejack is the oldest native distilled spirit in the United States. The Laird family has been producing it in New Jersey ever since William Laird arrived from County Fyfe, Scotland, more than three centuries ago in 1698. Laird may have been in whiskey in the old country, but given that grapes and grain (to make wine and whiskey) were hard to come by in the colonies, the drink of choice was hard cider or brandy distilled from apples.

Early stagecoach travelers looked forward to stopping for a jug at the Colts Neck Inn. The inn was built in 1717 by a member of the Laird clan right next door to the original distillery, at the intersection of County Roads 537 and 34.

The Laird family was very much in the spirit of the American Revolution. Robert Laird was a soldier under General Washington, and when Washington's army was camped nearby, as during the Battle of Monmouth, the Lairds did their bit to supply the thirsty troops with applejack. Washington himself was already a devotee of the beverage, having written the Lairds sometime prior to 1760 to get their recipe for "cyder," which he began producing on his own estate in Virginia. Martha Washington used applejack to flavor her walnut cake, and Thomas Jefferson added it to his sweet potato pie.

Apple brandy spread west to the Ohio River valley in the 1820s, thanks to an evangelist preacher named John Chapman, known as Johnny Appleseed. The product even appeared on a saloon license issued to Abraham Lincoln in 1833.

Laird & Company survived Prohibition by making sweet cider and apple brandy "for medicinal purposes." Based in Scobeyville, the company now produces 95 percent of all applejack sold in the United States, as well as a variety of other spirits. Today's applejack is still made from a variety of tree-ripened apples—including Delicious, Jonathan, Stayman, Pippin, and Winesap—that are pressed into sweet cider, fermented, distilled, and aged in charred oak barrels.

Laird's AppleJack:

This unique 80-proof blend of apple brandy and neutral grain spirits is a Jersey favorite.

new jersey when...

...you comb Lake Como but find no trace of George Clooney

There's not a single Italianate palazzo here, nor anyone you could mistake for George Clooney. That's because this Lake Como is not in Italy, where the Hollywood hunk prefers to spend his leisure time, but on the Jersey Shore.

Until recently you couldn't find the tiny borough of Lake Como on a single state map. The explanation for this bit of confusion is simple: The town of Lake Como was previously known as South Belmar. Now, "South Belmar" seems like a perfectly nice name; break down the *Bel* and *mar* portions of it, and you get "beautiful sea." So why, you may ask, did borough residents vote in November 2004 to change the name?

We suspect that one of the reasons was a quest for identity. Belmar proper is a well-known beach resort that gained something of a reputation for group summer rentals occupied by college students and other high-spirited youths. (Local residents complain often and loudly about "Animal House" behavior, which, though less than it was in the past, still exists.)

For all of that, Belmar has a great beach. South Belmar, a 0.20-square-mile borough of some 1,800 people squeezed between Belmar, Spring Lake, and Wall, does not have a single foot of beachfront. This made the notion of the "beautiful sea" something of a cruel joke for residents and visitors. It

> ### Lake Como:
> This Jersey Shore town was formerly known as South Belmar.

also irritated the heck out of the town clerk when folks called up looking for beach passes.

The borough does, however, border Lake Como, a very respectable body of water that lies between the town and posh Spring Lake. So Lake Como the town became—a return to roots, some residents said, for when the place was first developed back in the 1880s, it was actually known as Lake Como. We don't mind either way, as we're not the ones who have to print new return address labels.

you know you're in
new jersey when...
...wolves prowl at night—and not just in bars

There's no dancing with wolves at the Lakota Wolf Preserve, located high on the ridge of north Jersey's Kittatinny Mountains. In fact, the native wolf was long gone from these here hills, having been exterminated throughout the United States (with the exception of Alaska and Minnesota). But the preserve has given this feared predator a home in the East for the first time in more than a century.

Lakota (www.lakotawolf.com) is the labor of love of wildlife photographer Dan Bacon; his wife, Pam; and his partner, Jim Stein. Bacon first adopted a few wolf pups, which he kept in Colorado, but soon enough the pack outgrew its quarters and a more permanent arrangement had to be made. Thanks to the sale of Stein's house, Lakota was born.

Four tundra wolves, nine timber wolves, and nine arctic wolves now call this corner of New Jersey home; they reside in three separate compounds, one territory for each pack. Lakota also has a compound that houses wolf pups, bobcats, and foxes.

Wolf Watch, during which visitors can enter the observation area in the middle of the four compounds, takes place every morning and afternoon (except Monday) at Lakota. Visitors must wait for the wolves to come out of the woods, which they do most readily at feeding time. The animals

Lakota Wolf Preserve:

This preserve has given the native wolf a home in the East for the first time in more than a century.

play, interact with each other, and sometimes even howl. Caretakers talk about the wolves' social structure, their eating habits, and their interaction with humans. Visitors who fall in love with these beautiful animals have the opportunity to sponsor a wolf.

All of the wolves at Lakota were born and hand-raised in captivity, so they are friendly and affectionate with their guardians. But even they are far from domesticated, and visitors are warned not to imagine that this behavior can be found in the wild.

you know you're in
new jersey when...
...you finally see the light

With 127 miles of coastline and a seafaring history that goes back to 1609, when Henry Hudson sailed the *Half Moon* along the coast of New Jersey and into Sandy Hook Bay, the Garden State has plenty of history and lore to interest lighthouse-lovers.

Sandy Hook Lighthouse is the oldest working lighthouse in the United States, having first lit its original beacon of 48 whale oil lamps on June 11, 1764. Held by the British during the Revolutionary War, the octagonal white tower survived American cannon fire to shine its light on the bayshore for more than two centuries.

From Sandy Hook you can see the Highlands, which Hudson described in 1609 as "a very good land to fall in with, and a pleasant land to see." On the crest of the hill, you'll also see the Twin Lights of Navesink, a brownstone fortress with two castellated turrets that dates back to 1862. It's famous as the location of Guglielmo Marconi's first wireless telegraph antenna, which was erected atop the hill in 1899.

Two other New Jersey lighthouses also boast technological innovations. Sea Girt was the country's first lighthouse with a radio fog signal. And Barnegat Light's first-order Fresnel lens, a 12-foot-tall beehive structure of 1,024 prisms, produced a light so intense that it could be seen by ships up to 30 miles away and prevented many a wreck in the tricky waters off Barnegat Bay.

"Old Barney" leads a quiet life now, posing for so many photographers and painters that the 170-foot red-and-white tower has become a symbol of the Jersey Shore.

Though largely replaced by sonar, these beacons are certainly not forgotten. Each October the New Jersey Lighthouse Society (www.njlhs.org) organizes the Lighthouse Challenge. Aficionados try to hit all of the state's 11 land-based lighthouses in a day to collect an "11 Points of Light Club" souvenir. Three of the beacons—East Point, Finn's Point, and Tinicum—are not always open to the public.

What's the attraction, you ask? It's a day out, it's a part of local history, and, to paraphrase Freud, sometimes a lighthouse is just a lighthouse.

Lighthouses:

Sailors once relied on Jersey's lighthouses to get home safely. Now we go just for the view.

Most Americans today know all about the travails of Elizabeth Smart and the terrible JonBenet Ramsey murder. But few are old enough to remember the frenzy that gripped the country when the son of aviator Charles Lindbergh was kidnapped in New Jersey on a cold and rainy night.

After making the first solo flight across the Atlantic Ocean in 1927, Lindbergh became the media darling of his era—like Madonna and Neil Armstrong rolled into one. In 1929 "Lucky Lindy" married the beautiful Anne Morrow of Englewood Cliffs, and in 1930 Charles Jr. was born. To escape the ever-intrusive press, Lindbergh built a house on a 390-acre tract in a remote area near Hopewell in Mercer County.

Then the unthinkable happened: On March 1, 1932, the 20-month-old baby disappeared. A homemade wooden ladder was found outside his nursery window. The investigation—led by Colonel H. Norman Schwarzkopf, founder of the New Jersey State Police and father of General "Stormin' Norman"—was sidetracked by thousands of false leads and suspects and by the many outsiders (such as gangster Al Capone) who involved themselves.

In April 1932 the Lindberghs paid a $50,000 ransom. Nonetheless, in May the baby was found in a shallow grave not far from the Lindbergh home; he had been dead for quite some time.

In 1934 Bruno Hauptmann, a German immigrant, was caught spending some of the ransom money. His trial, held in the Hunterdon County Courthouse, was "the greatest story since the Resurrection" (according to H. L. Mencken). Reporters and spectators swarmed the small town. Hauptmann was condemned to death and executed in April 1936. His wife always maintained his innocence, and volumes have debated the fairness and the facts of the case.

Courtroom buffs can visit the historic courthouse in Flemington, which hosts a reenactment of the drama every fall (www.famous trials.com). And budding CSIs can examine the key evidence in the case, which is on display at the New Jersey State Police Museum and Learning Center in West Trenton (www.njsp.org/about/museum.html).

Lindbergh Baby Kidnapping:

This 1932 event in Hopewell was dubbed the "Crime of the Century."

you know you're in
new jersey when...
... you catch some rays in the shadow of Seven Presidents

With extreme condo and townhouse developments lining the oceanfront and beyond, Long Branch is now a bedroom community as well as a weekend getaway for New Yorkers. But once upon a time in the 19th century, it had a glamorous image as a veritable Monte Carlo at the Shore, with pristine beaches, posh gambling parlors, huge oceanfront hotels, and exciting horse races.

The list of "beautiful people" who vacationed in Long Branch is impressive: actors Edwin Booth, Lillie Langtry, and Lillian Russell; writers Bret Harte and Robert Louis Stevenson; artist Winslow Homer; and renowned man-about-town Diamond Jim Brady.

Though Mary Todd Lincoln visited in 1861, it was the post–Civil War era that made the resort a presidential getaway. Ulysses S. Grant established a summer White House in Long Branch, bringing in his wake other important people eager to escape Washington's intense heat. More presidents followed: Rutherford B. Hayes, James A. Garfield, Chester A. Arthur, Benjamin Harrison, William McKinley, and Woodrow Wilson, former governor of New Jersey.

Garfield, in fact, died in the Elberon section of Long Branch; a plaque on Garfield Terrace marks the spot. His funeral services were held at nearby St. James Chapel on Ocean Avenue, where he once worshipped.

Long Branch:

Seven presidents and numerous celebrities summered here, and it's still a nice getaway.

The other presidents worshipped there, too—hence the nickname "Church of the Presidents." The building fell into serious disrepair but is now being restored.

Though the presidents are long gone, the memory of past greatness lingers in street and building names like Lincoln, Grant, and Garfield. Seven Presidents Oceanfront Park, named for the chief executives who gave Long Branch its greatest cachet, is on the site of "The Reservation," built for the Buffalo Bill Wild West Show. The show featured Annie Oakley and Chief Sitting Bull, as well as the famous Bill Cody.

For kids who think that all food comes shrink-wrapped in plastic—and grown-ups who can't remember when it didn't—a visit to Longstreet Farm in Holmdel can be like a trip in a time machine.

Longstreet is one of the state's three living-history farms. Workers in period clothes till the soil with 19th-century tools, while other volunteers demonstrate old-fashioned methods of cooking and baking. Tours of the chicken house, corn crib, cow house, and potato house recall a time when putting food on the table took hours of serious labor. And the 30-foot well proves that getting a drink of water once took more effort than simply turning on a tap.

The farm, 495 acres assembled in 1806 by Hendrick Longstreet, was among the most prosperous farms in Monmouth County. It remained in the Longstreet family until the county purchased it in 1967.

The farmhouse, which was built in sections between 1775 and 1840, has 14 rooms. The nine public rooms speak of life as it was lived more than a century ago: Gentlemen retired to the back parlor after dinner for cigars and brandy, for example, and ladies might have written letters or played cards in the sitting room. The kitchen boasted such "modern" conveniences as apple peelers, egg poachers, fruit presses, and waffle

Longstreet Farm:

This living-history site proves that putting food on the table was once *really* hard work.

irons. It's enough to make you want to hug your microwave oven.

Longstreet also has blacksmiths who smith, quilters who quilt, and industrious people who do all kinds of chores. To sweeten up this vision of times gone by, there's an annual Halloween party. For more information, call 732–946–3758 or visit the Longstreet Farm page at www.monmouth countyparks.com.

Who wouldn't love Lucy? She is more than a century old, stands six stories tall, and weighs 90 tons; she has survived hurricanes, a fire, and years of neglect. Lucy the Elephant is a familiar sight to south Jersey beachgoers and was named to the National Register of Historic Places in 1971.

Conceived as an advertising gimmick by James Lafferty Jr., Lucy cost more than $25,000 to construct way back in 1881. Lafferty hoped that his whopping investment would attract buyers to the oceanfront lots he had for sale in the area south of Atlantic City now called Margate. Lucy was a success; the real estate venture flopped.

Lucy's next owner was Anthony Gertzen. In the 83 years that Lucy was part of the Gertzen family, she remained a tourist attraction—but she did come down in the world. After a 1903 hurricane she was moved 100 feet inland and turned into a tavern. A couple of years later, a fellow who couldn't hold his liquor knocked over a lantern and caused a fire that nearly burned Lucy to the ground. In 1929 she lost her howdah (the ribbed cage on her back) in a storm; she went on to weather even more hurricanes and Nor'easters in the decades that followed.

In 1970 the Gertzens donated Lucy to the city of Margate, which moved the elephant two blocks to the town's public beach at Decatur and Atlantic Avenues. Thanks to the Save Lucy Committee, restoration on the lovable elephant began; she now attracts about 30,000 visitors a year.

Lucy has her own Web site (www.lucythe elephant.org), where you can view photos of her interior and read about her history and unusual anatomy. In summer stop by the outdoor I Love Lucy Beach Grille for a sandwich or a soda.

Lucy the Elephant:

This 65-foot-tall wooden elephant towers over the savannahs of Margate.

you know you're in
new jersey when...
... you seek your fortune at the Temple of Knowledge

If you ever strolled the boardwalk during Asbury Park's better days, wandering from Convention Hall to the antique carousel, past Sandy's Arcade, the kiddie rides, the minigolf course, and Criterion Candies, then you know about Madame Marie— even if you never actually had the nerve to go in and have your fortune told.

Marie Costello opened her Temple of Knowledge back in the 1940s, when anxious women hoped for good news about their men overseas. She might have passed quietly into obscurity, along with the other boardwalk amusements, were it not for a skinny kid from Freehold who used to play guitar in a bar across the street called the Stone Pony.

"One day he decided to come in for a reading," Marie recalls, "and I told him he was going to be a success." The kid was Bruce Springsteen. On his second album, *The Wild, the Innocent & the E Street Shuffle* (1973), he immortalized Madame Marie in a song that evokes the sultry days and nights of summer at the Jersey Shore.

Contrary to the lyrics of "4th of July, Asbury Park (Sandy)," the cops never actually busted Madame Marie for telling fortunes better than they did. But thanks to The Boss, her reputation was made.

Madame Marie:

This fortune-teller predicted success for Bruce and a prosperous future for Asbury Park.

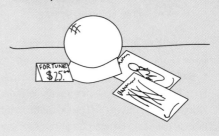

Marie returned to her old spot on the boardwalk in 2004 after a seven-year hiatus, the period of Asbury Park's steepest decline. Her quarters were repainted bright blue, and her sign was refurbished for a new generation of clients. Now in her 90s, Madame Marie once saw a prosperous future for Asbury Park. The Temple of Knowledge is going to be a part of it, as Marie's granddaughter has taken over the family fortune-telling business.

Need some tender loving care after a rough night out? Before you take this as an invitation to get hammered at a raucous Jersey Shore club, please keep in mind that this particular mission of mercy extends only to dolphins, whales, and other intelligent forms of life.

Established in 1978, the Marine Mammal Stranding Center and Sea Life Museum in Brigantine (www.marinemammalstranding center.org) gets reports of beached whales, disoriented dolphins, and animals that have been hit by boats. The center quickly dispatches rescue workers to do whatever is needed, whether it's returning an animal to deeper water or bringing it back to the center for medical care.

Staff and volunteers at the center, open since 1978, have been called out more than 3,000 times, with many gratifying results. Among the creatures they have rescued are a five-pound Kemp's Ridley sea turtle and a 25-ton humpback whale—both endangered species. One of the tiniest creatures rescued was a two-and-a-half-ounce loggerhead turtle hatchling. A staffer recalled, "He was so tiny, we had to weigh him on a postage scale." The turtle thrived and was eventually released. Not so lucky was a 66-ton finback whale that was D.O.A.

Rehabilitation for a single animal can last months and cost thousands of dollars, so this nonprofit organization is always in need of funds. One way to contribute is through the Adopt a Seal program. For $25 you can adopt a rehabilitating seal; after it is released, you will receive an adoption certificate, a photograph, and background information on how the seal was stranded and details about its recovery.

The center has a museum with photos of some of the more spectacular rescues, as well as a giant observation tank housing creatures that live in Jersey waters. The museum also has life-size replicas of game fish, sea turtles, and other marine mammals.

Marine Mammal Stranding Center:

This rehab center for whales, dolphins, seals, and sea turtles is located in Brigantine.

you know you're in
new jersey when...
...you hoist the mainsail and trim the jib

On busy summer weekends, when Jet Skis, fishing charters, and speedboats fill marinas with all the noise and traffic of the Jersey Turnpike, it's easy to forget the days when boating didn't require diesel fuel. Fortunately, the *A. J. Meerwald,* New Jersey's own tall ship, is here to remind us of a time when sailors charted a course by sextants and stars, not GPS.

The *Meerwald* (as it is usually called; www.ajmeerwald.org) is a 110-foot, two-masted 1928 schooner that has been authentically restored to serve as a maritime living-history museum. It is operated by the Bayshore Discovery Project.

Built by Charles H. Stowman & Sons, the *Meerwald* was one of hundreds of ships that came out of the boatyards along the shore of the Delaware Bay—before the Great Depression brought shipbuilding to a standstill. Commissioned by the Meerwald family of South Dennis as an oyster dredge, the schooner was typical in many ways of those built in this area, and its solid oak-on-oak construction saw it through half a century of hard labor.

During World War II the *Meerwald* was commandeered for service as a Coast Guard fireboat; it was motorized and stripped of its sailing rig. After the war the vessel was returned to the Meerwald family and used as an oyster dredge until 1957, when a parasite wiped out Jersey's oyster beds. The schooner was then outfitted for surf clamming until she was retired in the late 1970s.

Donated to the Delaware Bay Schooner Project in 1989, the ship was restored and refitted. In 1995 the *Meerwald* was named to the National Register of Historic Places, and in 1996 she was relaunched.

The *Meerwald* now travels from its home port of Bivalve to various ports statewide for special events and educational outings. Kids age 10 to 16 can be "sailors for a day" and learn to tie knots, hoist sails, swab the deck—and even take the helm. Those age 13 to 16 can enlist in "Maritime Camp," where they spend five days and four nights learning not only about being part of the crew of a tall ship, but also about environmental issues affecting the ocean.

The *Meerwald:*

The seagoing pride of the Garden State is a 1928 schooner.

you know you're in
new jersey when...
...Warhawks and Thunderbolts rule the wild blue yonder

In August 1941, months before the attack on Pearl Harbor, the Millville Airport in Cumberland County was designated "America's First Defense Airport"—so called because it was the first in a series of airfields nationwide dedicated to the defense of U.S. skies.

When war was declared Millville went into high gear. From 1942 to 1945 more than 10,000 men and women served there, with 1,500 pilots receiving advanced fighter training. Training began with the Curtiss P-40F "Warhawk," but after a few weeks the Republic P-47 "Thunderbolt" ruled the skies over Cumberland County.

Today, a large collection of World War II artifacts and memorabilia is displayed in the original base headquarters building. The history of the base and its important role in aviation is preserved at the Millville Army Air Field Museum (www.p47millville.org), which is dedicated to the men and women who served at the base and to the memory of the fourteen pilots who gave their lives while training there. With its rare artifacts and historic photos, the museum is a great complement to all the books and articles written about America's "Greatest Generation."

To further enrich the experience, World War II veterans usually lead tours. Millville also hosts air shows featuring historic aircraft, military jets, and acrobatic performers.

Millville Airport:

This airfield in Cumberland County was deemed "America's First Defense Airport."

On April 25, 1998, Millville's Wall of Remembrance—a mural that shows two versions of the Thunderbolt along with the image of a World War II fighter pilot—was dedicated to all who served in the war. A vintage Thunderbolt flew in tribute overhead.

you know you're in
new jersey when...
...there she goes, Miss America

After 84 years of a perfect union, the Miss America pageant and Atlantic City separated in 2005. Although the pageant has been criticized by feminists for objectifying women, its biggest enemy of late has been indifference. Organizers hoped to bolster sagging television ratings by moving to Vegas, where nothing is too glitzy or too kitschy and where the spectacle of all that wholesomeness on the hoof might find a more receptive audience.

Gone but not forgotten, Miss America is literally part of the City by the Sea. The two-block Miss America RoseWalk (along Michigan Avenue between Atlantic and Arctic) is illuminated with rose-colored lights and lined with commemorative plaques for each winner from 1921 to the present. Pageant winners still return here to leave their mark: In January 2006 Jennifer Berry of Oklahoma was crowned Miss America in Vegas; in February she traveled to A.C., where her plaque was unveiled.

Locals still remember when 100,000 people would turn out for the annual September parade along the boardwalk, calling out to the hopeful Misses, "Show us your shoes!" True to tradition, the contestants would display a bit of shapely leg and high heels that were spangled, bejeweled, or otherwise decorated to reflect their home states.

Shoe fans can view an extensive collection of Miss America footwear along with

Miss America:

Born in 1921 in Atlantic City, New Jersey, she took off for Vegas in 2005.

gowns, vintage photos, and other memorabilia at the Sheraton Atlantic City, once headquarters for the pageant. In front of the hotel is a bronze statue of former host Bert Parks, holding a crown at just the right height so that anyone can duck under it and have a Miss America moment. You'll find the Sheraton at 2 Miss America Way.

The pageant may have left A.C., but the official song still celebrates the city where the pageant was born:

There she is, Miss America
There she is, your ideal
The dreams of a million girls who are
  more than pretty
May come true in Atlantic City.

you know you're in
new jersey when...
... hermits come out of their shells

Miss America may have deserted Atlantic City for Las Vegas, but Miss Crustacean is here to stay. Each year in August, Ocean City's 2-mile boardwalk comes alive as throngs of visitors gather to watch what we believe is the world's only hermit crab beauty pageant.

Some say Miss Crustacean is a silly send-up of the more famous Miss America contest, whereas others are offended by the idea of subjecting innocent crabs to the same kind of ridiculous behavior displayed by humans. To those of us more interested in eating crabs than in rallying for their rights, it's a bit of harmless fun that's been going on for more than three decades.

We're not quite sure what the criteria are in choosing a winner; there is no swimsuit competition, nor is there a demonstration of social skills for selecting a Miss Congeniality. The crabs are, however, dressed up in elaborate costumes designed by their owners. Past standouts have included Crabpunzel, distinguished by flowing locks, and Crabopatra, who traversed the runway on a platform carried by toga-wearing bearers.

In addition to the pageant, past festivities have included a race and a wrestling exhibition with scripted trash talk between combatants Crabilla Monsoon and Hogan Hermit. And who could resist an Elvis

impersonator singing "You Ain't Nothin' but a Hermit Crab"?

Though there's usually a field of 50-odd hopefuls competing for the coveted Cucumber Cup, there can be only one winner—and she is serenaded with the classic "Here She Comes, Miss Crustacean." It's a wonder that there's a dry eye to be found on the boardwalk.

There is one minor glitch in this competition: No one seems able to state with certainty whether Miss Crustacean is actually a she or a he. Never mind; the judges are very liberal. And Jersey has a history of gender-bending (see page 58).

Miss Crustacean:

If you own an attractive hermit crab with a good wardrobe, bring her (or him) along to the annual Miss Crustacean Hermit Crab Beauty Contest in Ocean City.

you know you're in
new jersey when...
...boys will be boys—or maybe not

Back in the 1970s, when most tourists avoided Asbury Park, a queer thing (so to speak) happened. An underground gay nightlife began to emerge, starting with a few small clubs (like the Blue Note and Club Odyssey) that drew customers from both New York and Philadelphia.

In 1981 the owner of Club Odyssey, Ray Palazzo, started an event that outlived his business: the Miss Gay New Jersey Pageant. This annual drag queen contest is a charity event that benefits Beacon Light, an emergency fund for people diagnosed with HIV/AIDS. When the original venue closed, the pageant moved to other clubs before going big-time in 2001 and taking over such venues as the Sheraton Eatontown and the boardwalk Paramount Theater.

The pageant has become part of the annual Jersey Pride event, which takes place in June. This celebration boasts headliners like the Village People and may include a bowling tournament (Pins for Pride) or a poker tournament; crafters and food vendors; and a parade with floats, decorated vehicles, and hundreds of marchers.

Along the way Asbury has attracted a gay community of year-round residents and New Yorkers and Philadelphians who have bought second homes. It's been estimated that rainbow flags now fly from one house

Miss Gay New Jersey:

Goodbye, Miss America. Hello, handsome.

in five. In 2004 Deputy Mayor Jim Bruno even performed a same-sex marriage before the state shut him down.

All this may be shocking to some readers in the red states, but here in Jersey, where our neighbors come from every country and culture in the world, you have to do a lot more than wear women's clothing to outrage people—like, for instance, root for the Dallas Cowboys to beat the Giants.

you know you're in
new jersey when...
...you've completely lost your marbles

With all the "Gosh, Wally" innocence of *Leave It to Beaver,* the National Marbles Tournament (www.nationalmarbles tournament.org) is perfectly at home in Wildwood.

This Jersey Shore town is known for its boardwalk amusements and exuberant 1950s architecture (see page 25). But it's also renowned for the classic game it hosts each June. That's when boys and girls age 7 to 14, champion mibsters all, gather for four days to compete for the titles of King and Queen.

"Mibsters" are shooters or players. The game is Ringer—and it has nothing to do with cell phones. It's played by placing 13 marbles in the form of an X inside a 10-foot circle, with the contestants alternating shots. The winner is the first player to shoot seven marbles out of the ring.

Ringer Stadium consists of raised platforms set up on the beach, so weather plays an important role in the competition's outcome. If there has been rain, water on the game platform slows down the marbles and makes it harder to get a "stick." (That's when a shooter knocks out seven or more marbles in the first inning.) Windy days can bring sand into the equation.

About 1,000 matches are played during the course of the tournament, which dates

back to 1922, when it was originally sponsored by Macy's department store of Philadelphia. The game also gets its due in the Marbles Hall of Fame, which opened in 1993 in Wildwood's George F. Boyer Museum. Many tournament champions return each year to be officially inducted.

In addition to fame and glory, the kids compete for some $5,000 in scholarship money and other prizes. Of course, there are no losers here, as the kids all have a chance to cut loose on Wildwood's boardwalk, stuffing themselves with cotton candy and crashing around in the bumper cars.

National Marbles Tournament:

Each June in Wildwood, champion mibsters compete for money, prizes, and the titles of King and Queen.

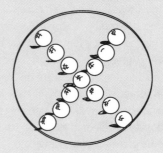

new jersey when...

... we all live in a naval submarine

Do you get claustrophobic just watching old World War II movies in which 100 men sealed in a submarine 50 fathoms down cringe with every depth charge? No? Then go to the New Jersey Naval Museum (www.njnm.com) in Hackensack and board the USS *Ling 297*.

The *Ling,* a 312-foot-long Balao-class submarine, was launched in 1943. She was the last of the fleet boats that patrolled America's shores looking for German U-boats. Decommissioned after World War II, she was towed to the Brooklyn Navy Yard in 1960, where she served as a training vessel.

In 1972 the *Ling* was saved from scrap by the Submarine Memorial Association, which had the ship brought to Hackensack to honor shipmates who had died in the war. Refurbished and authentically outfitted, the *Ling* is the star of the naval museum there.

We think that the *Ling* is an especially appropriate tribute, as the first submarine was invented just a few miles away by an Irish immigrant named John Holland. Convinced that submarines were the key to naval supremacy in the era of ironclads, Holland entered a Navy design contest. His proposal was rejected as "a fantastic scheme of a civilian landsman."

Undeterred, he built the *Holland No. 1* at Todd & Raftery's shop in Paterson. Com-

pleted in 1877, it was 14 feet long, carried one person, and was powered by a primitive 4-horsepower engine. Crowds awaited its launch in the Passaic River, but someone had forgotten to insert two screw plugs, and the sub began to sink. The following day, however, Holland made several successful dives.

The museum also has a movie star in its midst: the *Riverine,* a Vietnam War–era patrol boat seen in *Apocalypse Now.* As other vessels of this class have been stripped for parts, destroyed, or sold to foreign navies, the *Riverine* is the only one left in the northeastern United States. Also on display are the Japanese *Kaiten,* a suicide torpedo boat; a German *Seehund* (meaning "sea-dog" or "seal"); and a World War II two-man coastal sub.

New Jersey Naval Museum:

The USS *Ling* and other historic boats are preserved at this Hackensack shrine to naval history.

you know you're in
new jersey when...

... you root, root, root for the home team, but it's from another state

It's been more than 20 years since both the New York Giants and the New York Jets started playing their home games in East Rutherford, but neither team has ever shown the slightest interest in taking our name. The Jets even insist on commuting to games all the way from Hempstead, Long Island. Is that any way to treat the state that gave birth to the sport of football more than a century ago?

Students of the game know that the first college football game was played on November 9, 1869, in New Brunswick. The competitors were Queen's College (now Rutgers University) and the College of New Jersey (now more effetely known as Princeton). Each team had 25 men wearing no helmets or other special equipment. With one point scored for every touchdown, Rutgers won 6–4, but Princeton took the rematch a week later 8–0. This intrastate rivalry continued for more than 100 years, until Rutgers became a Division I school.

On the professional level, New Jersey's fan loyalty is divided. Italians almost invariably are true-blue to the tradition-rich Giants, whereas the Jets seem to draw the support of Irish-Americans, who perhaps are attracted to the green-and-white color scheme. Of course, venture south of Trenton, and it's Philadelphia Eagles territory.

Do these loyal and vocal fans feel slighted that both franchises cling to a perhaps

New York Giants and New York Jets:

You can call yourself what you want, but what plays in Jersey stays in Jersey.

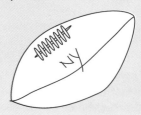

more prestigious address? By and large, no; after all, half of us moved here from New York, too. Just keep the games right here in Giants Stadium. (Not that it's exactly paradise, what with the wind, traffic jams, and outrageously priced parking, watery beer, and second-rate hot dogs.)

What did make fans nervous was New York City's proposed multibillion-dollar Westside stadium project, which threatened to lure one, if not both, teams back to the city. Officials already managed to shanghai the Nets to be sales bait for a huge real estate development in Brooklyn—now that they're finally winning. But the Westside plan went nowhere, and now it seems that the Giants and Jets will be sharing a "new and improved" Meadowlands Stadium—if it ever happens.

Born in Neptune on April 22, 1937, John Joseph Nicholson was raised believing that his grandmother was his mother and his mother was his older sister. *Chinatown?* No, just Jersey. He learned the truth in 1974, when a *Time* researcher checked the facts of his birth for a story on the star.

After graduating from Manasquan High School, where he was voted Class Clown and Best Actor, Nicholson went to Hollywood to work as a messenger in MGM's cartoon department. He later worked for Roger Corman, the king of low-budget movies. The 1969 biker flick *Easy Rider* earned the Jersey gigolo the first of his record 12 Academy Award nominations.

With his circumflex eyebrows and ever-so-slightly menacing grin, Nicholson gave style and panache to Batman's favorite nemesis, the Joker. His larger-than-life persona also seemed eminently suited to the film *A Few Good Men;* his memorable delivery of "You can't handle the truth!" made the line part of everyday parlance.

Combining his devilish good looks with a convincing talent for playing crazy people garnered the veteran actor Oscars for *One Flew Over the Cuckoo's Nest* and *As Good As It Gets.* And who else could have made the line "Heeeeere's Johnny!" so terrifying in *The Shining?*

Nicholson, Jack:

As of 2006, this Neptune-born actor had won 3 Oscars and received 12 nominations.

Unlike some Hollywood stars, Nicholson stays in touch with his Jersey roots. One former classmate spotted Jack with actress Lara Flynn Boyle; another noted that the star sent flowers when a high school classmate died. In 2004 Nicholson attended his 50th high school reunion at the Riverview Pavilion in Belmar, delighting many by remembering names and faces. He presented fellow alumni with a CD set of '50s music, with a caricature of himself printed on the side.

you know you're in
new jersey when...
... you can be a child again

When you build it, kids will come. That's what happened when Bruce Williams and his wife, Jean, began a 24-year-long labor of love in 1972.

It started while their first house was being built in Flemington. After the construction crew left each night, Bruce would retreat to the basement to work on what would become the Great American Railway. It is the world's largest model railroad, with 135 trains and 8 miles of track, 35-foot mountains and 40-foot bridges, thousands of handcrafted buildings, and more than 10,000 freight cars.

Williams—a concert musician, entrepreneur, award-winning computer software developer, and publisher—didn't stop there. Giving his imagination full rein, he kept right on building, creating the La Peep Dollhouse, a 94-room miniature mansion that even Barbie would envy, complete with an indoor swimming pool and a two-story library.

Then came the Raritan River Railway, a two-thirds-scale steam replica that travels through tunnels and over bridges; the Doll Museum, which houses more than 200 collectible dolls from around the world; and the Music Hall, where a 2,000-pipe organ that offers several concerts each day is the centerpiece of a 500-seat theater.

Kids of all ages love the complex, called Northlandz (www.northlandz.com). Not only are there wondrous things to see and hear, but there is also kid-licious stuff to eat: The Club Car serves pizza, hot dogs, ice cream, popcorn, muffins, and cookies. As you might expect, Northlandz has gotten a lot of media attention in newspapers and magazines, as well as on CNN and various other television networks.

Northlandz:

This entertainment complex in Flemington is home to the Great American Railway, among other kid-friendly attractions.

Back in 1869, a group of Methodist ministers on the Jersey Shore decided that they wanted a healthful and spiritual summer retreat. They aimed to escape the debauchery of nearby Long Branch, where swells like Diamond Jim Brady came to gamble, drink liquor, and carouse with loose women.

And so Ocean Grove was founded. Members of the National Camp Meeting Association for the Promotion of Holiness arrived at this lovely oceanfront area the following summer, pitched their tents, and attended prayer services held in the great outdoors.

The spirit of the camp meeting endures, and the tents still reappear every summer. Crowded one right next to another, they take up the entire green between the Great Auditorium and the ocean. Privacy is not the order of the day here, as entire families share the same tent year after year. The tents rent for a few thousand dollars each, but the waiting list averages 10 years— longer than season tickets for the Giants!

To keep things on the straight and narrow, the Association banned alcohol and later, driving a car on Sunday. It also kept beach entrances closed until noon on Sunday to avoid the temptations of sun and surf during services. The blue laws were strictly enforced up to 1974. Until then, you also had to have a reference from a Methodist minister to "buy" a house in Ocean Grove. (And you thought co-op boards were

tough!) Technically, the church owns the land—homeowners are given a 99-year lease.

The center of social activities in Ocean Grove is the Great Auditorium, a stunning 1894 wooden hall that holds about 6,000 people. In the past folks crowded in to hear famous preachers such as Billy Graham and Norman Vincent Peale. Nowadays, acts like Peter, Paul & Mary; Al Martino; and the Preservation Hall Jazz Band appear during the summer season.

Main Street now boasts chic new eateries, and many of the old Victorian guesthouses have been bought and refurbished by enterprising gay couples from the City. Although the new arrivals have been known to drink wine and play music on the Sabbath, the town's small-time charm endures.

Ocean Grove:

Founded in 1869, this Methodist retreat on the Jersey shore still holds summer camp meetings.

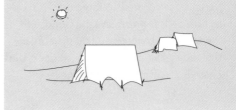

you know you're in
new jersey when...
...vintage architecture is Paramount

Asbury Park's Paramount Theater is an art deco treasure, a commanding presence on the boardwalk adjoining Convention Hall. In its heyday the Paramount hosted gala, star-studded movie premieres, but it suffered from neglect in the 1970s and 1980s. The theater is such a part of Asbury history that everyone at the Shore was glad when in 1996 the state earmarked funds for structural repairs. Though not exactly restored to its former glory, the Paramount is once again a great place to take in a concert.

But even preservation-minded locals would probably be surprised to learn that another great old Paramount Theater languishes under detritus and coats of paint just a few miles down the road. It's in Long Branch, hiding behind the sickly green façade of Siperstein's Paint and Decorating Store.

Vintage postcards show the ornate theater as it was back in the 1930s, when it was called "The Broadway," after Long Branch's main street. Sadly, the theater closed in the late 1950s; the last film to play there was *Middle of the Night,* starring Fredric March and Kim Novak. Eventually the building was taken over by Siperstein's and used for storage.

If owner Todd Katz is of a mind to show you his faded treasure, a fantastic sight will greet your eyes. The enormous auditorium, which had more than 1,700 seats, is filled with thousands of paint cans stacked high.

Paramount Theater:

This dusty treasure in Long Branch promises to soon shine as brightly as its Asbury Park counterpart.

There's also a splendid balcony, chandeliers crusted with dust (think *Phantom of the Opera*), and elaborate plaster decorations covered with flaking gilt. The place is like the ghost of a more glamorous time.

Now, after a few years of eminent domain abuse, Long Branch is in the middle of a real estate boom, and there are plans to revitalize Broadway and the Paramount. The Broadway Arts project calls for shops, restaurants, and hundreds of residential units, some set aside for artists, students, and affordable housing. There will be two theaters: the restored Paramount and a new home for the New Jersey Repertory Company, with a developer promising to spend $7.1 million on improvements to both.

you know you're in
new jersey when...
...you take two pills and go to work in the morning

Texas has oil, and Michigan has cars. New Jersey has pills. Few people outside the medical profession know that pharmaceutical production, research, and development make up the state's largest manufacturing industry. In fact, the Garden State has been called "the world's medicine cabinet," producing 40 percent of all medications sold worldwide.

Home to more sophisticated global pharmaceutical companies than any other state or country in the world, Jersey hosts a list of firms that reads like a stock ticker: Johnson & Johnson, Bristol Myers-Squibb, Merck, Hoffman-La Roche, Schering-Plough, Novartis, Wyeth, Ortho-McNeil, Hoechst-Aventis—and even ImClone, whose stock landed Martha Stewart in the slammer. Of course, most of these companies are international conglomerates, but quite a few have their roots in Jersey.

Modern pharmaceutical manufacturing was established here in the early 1900s, and pioneering New Jersey companies are credited with a number of drug breakthroughs, including ether, sulfa drugs, synthetic cortisone, Valium, Librium, synthetic vitamins, streptomycin, and the mass-production of penicillin.

Today, research and development is under way in fields such as Alzheimer's disease, heart disease, AIDS, diabetes, and arthritis, as well as more than 50 other conditions.

Pharmaceuticals:

Jersey's got your cure right here.

So whether you suffer from ED or PMS or ADD, Jersey has just what the doctor ordered.

The manufacture of pharmaceuticals and medical devices creates billions of dollars in economic activity across the state, which translates to tens of thousands of stable, high-paying jobs for residents. How did the Garden State develop such an important industry? Analysts point to a number of factors: a talented, highly educated, and well-trained workforce; an excellent quality of life that's attractive to employees; easy access to major transportation; and proximity to Wall Street capital.

So next time you pour yourself some water to wash down those meds, raise your glass to Jersey.

you know you're in
new jersey when...
... you pine for the green, green grass of home

We should say right away that the Pine Barrens are not at all barren. Dutch settlers came up with this misleading appellation because the high pH of the soil made it impossible for them to grow their traditional crops. (Cranberries and blueberries do very well in the Pine Barrens, also known as the Pinelands.)

New Jersey, the most densely populated state in America, also shelters 1.1 million acres of forested coastal plain that sprawl over eight southern and central counties and make up about one-fifth of the entire state. Designated a biosphere reserve by the United Nations, this acreage is the largest tract of open space east of the Mississippi.

And what a wondrous place it is! Here you'll find the rarest of plants, like the federally protected swamp pink lily, the exotic lady slipper orchid, and the bog asphodel, which is found nowhere else in the world. Thirty-nine animals facing extinction in Jersey—including the barred owl, the northern pine snake, and the tiny (1.5-inch) Pine Barrens tree frog—also make their home in the Pinelands.

But it isn't just exotic flora and fauna that have lived here. During the American Revolution the Pinelands sheltered deserting soldiers, British loyalists, and the notorious outlaws known as the Pine Robbers. Some of the Robbers were disgruntled British sailors who had jumped ship and joined with local outlaws to do their dastardly pillaging and killing. Thanks to Captain Sam Allen (a cousin of Ethan Allen), a number of Pine Robbers were caught and hanged.

Nowadays, the Pinelands are home to regular people known as Pineys. Granted, others use the name in a derogatory way, insinuating that Pineys are, well, not quite as bright as they could be. (A genetic study was once conducted to test this premise; it's not true.) But the Pineys themselves wear the name proudly, secure in the knowledge that they have the best of all possible worlds.

And, oh yes, the Jersey Devil (see page 38) is said to live in the Pinelands. During the Halloween season the Pinelands Preservation Alliance (www.pinelandsalliance.org) conducts Jersey Devil hunts—if you dare.

Pine Barrens:

Designated a "Last Great Space" by the Nature Conservancy, the Pine Barrens are home to endangered species—and the Jersey Devil.

you know you're in
new jersey when...
... your goodwyfe fetches you a drink of water

It was at the Battle of Monmouth that Molly Pitcher became legend as the lady with the cool drinks. This key battle in the American Revolution took place in June 1778 during a brutal heat wave. With the British retreating across New Jersey, General George Washington's Continental Army engaged the enemy at Freehold (now Battlefield State Park). After hours of fighting, men on both sides collapsed from heat exhaustion.

It was then that Molly Pitcher earned her moniker, showing the can-do spirit of Jersey Girls throughout the centuries. Molly, aka Mary Ludwig Hays, was married to Pennsylvania artilleryman William Hays and followed his unit into battle. Through the smoke and the noise, Mary ran from the Continental lines to a nearby well, fetching water for the soldiers to drink—and to cool down the cannon barrels as they became overheated.

When Mary's husband fell (whether from the heat or a wound), she took his place at the cannon and held it, helping to avert a Continental retreat. One story claims that after the battle, General Washington made her a noncommissioned officer—and that she was known thereafter as Sergeant Molly.

Some historians maintain that Molly Pitcher is more fiction than fact, simply a generic nickname given to all the brave women who carried water to the fighting men during the American Revolution. Others say that her story actually combines details from the lives of two women—our Mary and a Margaret Corbin. But to us, it's all about Mary.

Not far from the Battle of Monmouth site is a hotel called the Molly Pitcher Inn; there's also a rest stop on the Jersey Turnpike bearing her name. In 1928 her name was overprinted on the 2-cent postage stamp. And during World War II, the Liberty ship SS *Molly Pitcher* was launched; sadly, she was torpedoed in 1943.

Pitcher, Molly:

This Jersey Girl made a name for herself at the Battle of Monmouth.

you know you're in
new jersey when...
... you get reelected from your jail cell

We admit it: Jersey is known for political shenanigans. Our own residents suggested that the state motto be "New Jersey: Most of Our Elected Officials Have Not Been Indicted." Unfortunately, many have—and to read our local papers, it seems that some mayor or councilman is headed for jail every other week. In the city of Camden alone, a tally a few years ago showed that three out of the last five mayors had been indicted.

Yet not all miscreants have been forced out of politics; some have been forgiven by a public that likes them in spite of their transgressions. A classic example: In 1982 Mayor William V. Musto of Union City was running for a seventh term, even though he'd been charged with 36 counts of racketeering that could have landed him in prison for up to 20 years. The popular mayor was found guilty, and 24 hours after he was sentenced to seven years, Musto handily won reelection.

In the same year, Newark mayor Kenneth A. Gibson finished first in his bid for a fourth term—though he had been indicted on charges relating to the creation of a no-show city job. Lacking a majority of votes, Gibson faced a runoff against Earl Harris, president of the city council, who had been indicted on the same charges. Gibson got his fourth term and an acquittal, though he was later indicted (and pled guilty) to

Political Scandals:

Jersey has its fair share of elected officials who have broken the law—not that it hurts them at the polls.

charges of defrauding the school board of Irvington.

Sometimes, however, the public just shakes its collective head at elected lawbreakers. In 1994 Mayor Kenneth Buckley of Asbury Park was arrested for making a drug buy in a bar across the street from City Hall. Turns out the buy was really a sting by local, state, and federal prosecutors. Buckley resigned a few months later. Had he finished his term and run again, we suspect that he might not have been reelected, as folks were heard to say, "Did he have to buy drugs across the street from City Hall? Now that is *really* dumb."

you know you're in
new jersey when...
...breakfast is a hearty P.E.C.

Peruse the menu at almost any Jersey diner, and you'll probably see something called a P.E.C. going for two bucks and change. What exactly is a P.E.C., you out-of-staters may ask? It's a pork roll, egg, and cheese sandwich on a kaiser roll, also known as a heart attack on a plate.

Pork roll, aka Taylor ham, is an indigenous Jersey creation that may date back as far as the 1700s. What we know for sure is that the "Original Taylor Ham" comes from the Taylor Provision Company of Trenton and is sold in Garden State supermarkets.

Until recently, this artery-clogging treat was largely unavailable beyond New York City and Philadelphia. But we understand that the Publix markets in Florida now carry Taylor Pork Roll, probably for the large number of snowbirds who cannot wait until spring for their next grease fix. Safeway supermarkets in the Washington, D.C., area sell it, too, perhaps at the request of homesick Congressional staffers. Jersey expats anywhere else can now satisfy their cravings via the Internet, as several online retailers will ship the beloved pork product wherever it's most desperately needed.

In our nitrite-phobic, fat-gram-counting age, can this Jersey favorite get the recognition it deserves? Probably not, but natives like movie director Kevin Smith and rock star Jon Bon Jovi are doing their best to let the

Pork Roll, Egg, and Cheese:

This hearty Jersey breakfast sandwich features Taylor ham and a week's worth of fat and calories.

rest of America know what they're missing. In a *Playboy* interview Bon Jovi said: "Taylor ham—a pork roll—is a Jersey fixture. Taylor ham with cheese on a hard roll is love. The big question is: ketchup or mustard? Everyone in north Jersey puts on mustard, everyone in the south, ketchup."

new jersey when...

... you're no Einstein, but you can follow in his footsteps

The Ivy-est of the Ivy League colleges, Princeton was chartered in 1746 as the College of New Jersey. It is the oldest institute of higher education in the state and the fourth-oldest in the country. Locals grumble that it's only out-of-staters who go there, and indeed, with the exception of Supreme Court Justice Samuel Alito Jr., we had to go all the way back to Grover Cleveland and Aaron Burr to come up with any distinguished Jersey natives who have called it their alma mater.

The university does, however, boast a close association with Albert Einstein. As a young man Einstein set the discipline of science on its ear with his theory of relativity. He followed with the famous equation $E=mc^2$, which proposed that atomic mass could be converted to energy. After fleeing his native Germany on the eve of Hitler's ascension, Einstein found a physical and intellectual sanctuary at Princeton's Institute for Advanced Study.

Einstein became an American citizen and spoke out for such causes as civil rights and for the creation of the Jewish state of Israel, which promptly offered him its presidency (he declined, politely). He died in 1955 at Princeton Hospital; according to his wishes, his brain was removed for research purposes and remains at a secret Jersey location.

Einstein himself was a quiet, modest man who said, "My life is a simple thing that would interest no one." So he couldn't resist poking fun at the rarefied air Princetonians seem to breathe. He once called the town's leading lights "demigods on stilts."

The town bears no grudge. Stroll past old Nassau Hall to Landau's store on Nassau Street, and you'll find the nation's only museum dedicated to Einstein. Beyond the sale racks of scarves and sweaters is a collection of Einstein memorabilia: pictures, letters, stamps, newspaper articles, and even a seat cushion. A 1951 letter from a young girl reads as follows: "Dear Mr. Einstein, I am a little girl of six. I saw your picture in the paper. I think you ought to have your hair cut, so you can look better. Cordially yours, Ann G. Kocin."

Princeton:

This lovely university town was home to Albert Einstein from 1933 until his death in 1955.

$$e = mc^2$$

new jersey when...

...you get the blues and pop a bottle of blueberry bubbly

We have to hand it to Jersey ingenuity, displayed at its slightly bent best in the history of Renault Winery. Founded in 1864, Renault is the biggest and most popular of the state's wineries; it is also the only one that has managed to continue operating without interruption since the day it opened.

While Prohibition effectively shut down all other wineries, Renault was bought by John D'Agostino, who figured out ways to keep the place open. First, he got a dispensation to make sacramental wines for the church. Then he created a "new" product: a line of "tonics" that claimed to cure backaches and other ailments—and coincidentally happened to be 44-proof alcohol, along with a sour-tasting additive called peptone.

The label for these new patent "medicines," a clever marketing device if ever there was one, carried a "warning" to consumers: Do not refrigerate the tonic, or it will become wine. (When the product was chilled, the peptone would separate out.) The tonics were available at drugstores all over the United States. As you might imagine, they took off like a rocket and kept Renault operating and prospering when competitors nationwide disappeared.

Nowadays, Renault offers another, much tastier innovation: blueberry Champagne. No doubt cork dorks and wine snobs will sneer at the very name, but an honest taste could change their minds. For this sublime creation—Jersey's answer to the mimosa and Bellini—Renault blends blueberry juice with white Champagne that has been aged. The result: a bubbly azure drink with a distinct berry bite that has won an impressive array of prizes. (Alas, the winery uses Maine berries, which are supposedly smaller and more flavorful than Jersey's own fruit.)

In addition to winery tours and tastings, the Renault Winery in Egg Harbor (www.renault winery.com) now has a resort hotel with a golf course, a gourmet restaurant, and plans for a spa.

Renault Winery:

In continuous operation since 1864, this Jersey winemaker is known for its blueberry Champagne.

Ripley's Believe It or Not! museums have been wowing people with their collections of strange, often tacky stuff since 1933, when the first "Odditorium" made its debut at the Chicago World's Fair. Since then millions have *oohed* and *aahed* and *eewed* at the holdings of Ripley's museums all over the world, from Thailand to Denmark, England, and Mexico—and New Jersey, of course.

Located on the Atlantic City boardwalk, the Jersey museum lives right up (or down) to company standards. Where else could you see what's billed as the Jersey Devil's skeleton? Or the world's largest model of a suspension bridge, made of 160,000 toothpicks?

For history buffs, there is a lock of George Washington's hair. For kids who like to be grossed out, there's a collection of shrunken heads. And for lovers of the weird (pretty much anyone who pays admission), there is a fertility statue that looks exactly like what it's meant to be.

One exhibit that is exclusive to the Atlantic City museum is a roulette wheel made entirely of jelly beans. All of this seems perfectly at home amid the other boardwalk attractions. The museum is open daily, year-round. For more information, call 609–347–2001.

Ripley's Believe It or Not! Museum:

Step inside this Atlantic City attraction to view truly weird exhibits.

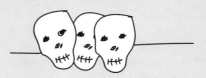

you know you're in
new jersey when...
...you drive by giants, Vikings, cowboys, and bears

On any given Sunday, Giants, Vikings, Cowboys, and/or Bears may be on view at the Meadowlands; but they're also larger-than-life figures along the highways and byways of the Garden State.

Our giant, also known as the Muffler Man and Paul Bunyan, has been enjoying his 15 minutes of fame since 1998, when he began appearing in the credits of *The Sopranos*. Located in front of Wilson's Carpet and Furniture, under the Pulaski Skyway in Jersey City, the figure is visible (if not entirely intelligible) to PATH train commuters. Originally located on Hoboken Avenue, he started out as a sort of lumberjack and later was handed a green steel roll to advertise carpet.

The helmeted Viking on Route 77 in Deerfield and the grinning cowboy outside Cowtown on Route 40 have not yet been discovered by Hollywood. Space Farm's Goliath, on the other hand, was recognized in his lifetime as the world's largest bear by the *Guinness Book of World Records*. Now stuffed, this Sussex wonder is no smaller.

Under the Holland Tunnel viaduct in Jersey City lies what locals unofficially call the world's largest cat: The fiberglass feline is 19 feet long and weighs more than 500 pounds. In the 1950s it enjoyed a moment in the sun as part of a float in the Macy's Thanksgiving Day Parade, but its retirement has been a bit of a letdown.

Roadside Attractions:

Jersey's highways and byways are home to a vast array of larger-than-life, often bizarre creatures.

It seems that New Jersey has quite a history of bizarre roadside displays. While most of them (like Margate's Lucy the Elephant) started out as some sort of attention-getting advertisement, there are plenty of cases of private citizens expressing themselves similarly. Josephine Stapleton of Mays Landing uses colored water to create designs—rainbows, American flags, Christmas themes—right on her front lawn. Less clear is the meaning of the absurdist assemblage of billboards and signs along Route 206 known as the Fabulous Fifty Acres.

Just keep your eyes on the road when encountering for the first time the hubcap pyramid on Route 322 in Weymouth or the slinky, 18-foot-tall Miss Uniroyal on Route 168 in Blackwood.

you know you're in
new jersey when...
...your life is a roller coaster

Life in Jersey is filled with ups and downs, and for many of us, there's nothing that mocks Fortuna like leaving your stomach at the top of a 60-foot drop. We're not talking about high-speed Himalayas or upside-down centrifuges—all that senseless spinning. No, the king of the rides remains the roller coaster.

At the Shore we start young on kid-size coasters like the Tornado and the Flitzer, both at Jenkinson's in Point Pleasant Beach. Then we move up to adventures like the Star Jet at Seaside Heights, a mile-long ride that reaches speeds of 40 miles per hour. Its 45-foot drop occurs at the end of the pier, while you're looking straight down at the ocean.

Roller coasters were not invented in Jersey (or on Coney Island, as many people think). They actually originated in France in the late 1700s and were called "Russian mountains," in honor of the ice slides that inspired their design.

Coaster aficionados get into the wood-versus-steel debate: Purists favor vintage wooden rides, while thrill-seekers hum to the speed, loops, and corkscrew twists that steel can create. Jersey has both. Morey's Piers in Wildwood has seven coasters, including the Great White. And in 2006 Six Flags in Jackson (Great Adventure to Jerseyans) opened El Toro, the second-tallest and second-fastest wooden coaster in the

United States. Its 76-degree drop generates a speed of 70 miles per hour.

Six Flags already had an impressive array of thrillers, including the tallest and fastest coaster on earth, the Kingda Ka. It launches riders from 0 to 128 miles per hour in 3.5 seconds before catapulting them 45 stories (458 feet) into the sky. That outdoes the 415-foot-tall Magic Mountain, which goes up to 100 miles an hour.

More Great Adventure coasters offer still other thrills—riding in the dark or without a floor. On Superman Ultimate Flight, riders lie down to hurtle head-first through a twisting steel track, diving through spirals and a pretzel-shaped inverted loop. Anything for truth, justice, and the American way.

Roller Coasters:

Prolific in Jersey, these rides may be the only place in the state you can travel at high speeds with no traffic.

you know you're in
new jersey when...
... surf's up

Ever since barefoot hippies discovered peace, love, and surfing at the Jersey Shore, Ron Jon T-shirts have been familiar sightings. Yet many of us longboard illiterates didn't realize that this iconic shop is right here in Ship Bottom.

For decades Ron Jon has been the Stone Pony of surfing—headquarters for everything that's going on at the Shore. Surfboards first appeared on this coast in the 1940s, but even through the 1950s, would-be Jersey surfers had to make their own boards or buy them on the West Coast.

Young Ron DiMenna was one of them; he loved to surf, but he was tired of making do with homemade boards. In 1959 he discovered the sublime pleasures of the fiberglass board and wanted one—a custom surfboard from California.

When he asked his dad for the money, the savvy senior DiMenna replied, "Buy three; sell two—and yours will be free." And that's how the first Ron Jon Surf Shop began on beautiful Long Beach Island. The shop's success made quality surfboards available to a much wider group of kids, and the popularity of surfing grew rapidly.

That store has become world-famous; it's now a four-floor emporium that carries everything you could possibly need for the surf, the beach, and the nautical-themed home.

Success followed success: Ron Jon has stores in California (Orange County) and Florida (Cocoa Beach, Fort Lauderdale, Key West, and Orlando), as well as an Internet shopping service (www.ronjons.com).

There's also a Ron Jon Surfpark in Orlando, where surfers can ride man-made waves when Nature doesn't supply any; a Ron Jon Resort in Cape Canaveral; and, through licensing agreements, Ron Jon shops in various airports and in Cozumel.

Ron Jon Surf Shop:

Jersey Shore native Ron DiMenna has proved that it's possible to succeed in business by doing what you love.

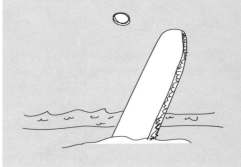

... nothing says "Wish You Were Here" like a box of sticky candy

Atlantic City has bragging rights to lots of good stuff, not the least of which is saltwater taffy. Though both salt and water are ingredients in this sticky candy, it is not, and never has been, made with salt water.

According to the story we've heard most often, the name came about in 1883, when the taffy was a recent invention and a candy stand owned by David Bradley was drenched by seawater during a storm. The following day, a child asked to buy some taffy, and Bradley replied, "You mean saltwater taffy, don't you?"

The name stuck—as does the candy. While Bradley's smart remark may have sparked a phenomenon, it was Joseph Fralinger who cashed in on it. As individual pieces of taffy were selling for a penny apiece or six for a nickel, Fralinger got the bright idea of selling the candy in boxes, packaged as souvenirs that tourists could take home.

Fralinger's business took off, but he soon had competition in the person of Enoch James, a candy maker from the Midwest who heard about the "taffy rush" and set up shop on the A.C. boardwalk. James's contribution to the taffy industry was a pulling machine that spared human hands from having to stretch the sticky stuff.

Saltwater Taffy:

This sticky candy was invented and popularized in Atlantic City.

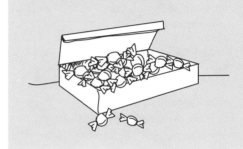

Though some claim that James's candy is creamier, both brands have their devotees. (Dentists across the country may have a different view of taffy, as they have this popular candy to thank for any number of displaced fillings among their patients.)

you know you're in
new jersey when...
...everyone in the state gets crabby

When you live in a state with 127 miles of coastline, you're never far from your next fried flounder. And though you don't really need more of an excuse than Saturday night to drive down the Shore for a great lobster dinner, in Jersey there's a festival for every appetite.

In April the seafood-celebration season kicks off in Belmar with the New Jersey Seafood Festival. More than 30 of the Shore's top restaurants share their finest fin fare alongside representatives of the state's viticulturists, who show off their vintages at the wine-tasting tent. The feast is tempered with arts and crafts, model boat demonstrations, environmental exhibits, and live jazz and blues music, plus a petting zoo and pony rides for the kids.

In mid-June the annual New Jersey Fresh Seafood Festival takes place in the historic Gardner's Basin section of Atlantic City. For two full days, the marina area is a family playground, with dozens of vendors offering a succulent selection of ocean fare. Cajun fried shrimp, clams and oysters on the half shell, various crab dishes, and chowders and soups are among the choices. There's music and entertainment—and when the last finger-licking morsel has been consumed, there's often the bonus of a gorgeous sunset.

The Baymen's Clam Bake in "Tip" Seaman Park (Ocean County Park) also takes place

Seafood Festivals:

Look no farther than your favorite Shore town for a good excuse to eat fish, drink beer, and have a good time.

in June. Here you'll find hot dogs and pork barbecue for those who don't like seafood.

Fun is always on the menu at the late-summer Barnegat Crab Race and Seafood Festival in Seaside Heights. If you have no desire to race a crab, you might come to eat one: Steamed crabs and other delicacies are on offer, not to mention entertainment, a craft fair, and a pageant for kids.

Summer's end is celebrated in Beach Haven with the Chowderfest Weekend, where tasters can debate the burning question "Manhattan or New England?" to their hearts' content. Live music accompanies the slurping, with various entertainment offerings for kids. For exact dates, check the Visitor Info section at www.discover southernocean.com.

you know you're in
new jersey when...
...you find yourself back on Shad Roe

Joni Mitchell once sang, "You don't know what you've got till it's gone." This is certainly true of shad, an unprepossessing member of the herring family that was abundant in New Jersey from the earliest colonial times. At the beginning of the 20th century, the shad catch on the Delaware River was the largest on the Atlantic Coast, but industrialization around Philadelphia and along the Raritan River led to water pollution, and eventually the shad all but disappeared.

The Clean Water Act of 1972 was the start of many cleanup and conservation efforts that slowly brought this seafaring harbinger of spring back to Jersey. Like salmon, shad spend most of their lives in the ocean, but they return to the freshwater river where they were hatched to swim upstream and spawn.

It took a while for the shad population to recover and return to the Delaware River, especially since it takes females from four to six years to reach reproductive maturity. But return they did, and in 1981 Lambertville (www.lambertville.org), which has a long shad-fishing history, inaugurated the Shad Festival to celebrate their homecoming.

For a whole weekend in April, natives and visitors alike are "mad about shad." They sing about it, speechify about its glorious reappearance, crown a Shad Queen, and watch demonstrations of skeining—the technique for catching shad. But most of all, everyone eats plenty of shad, fortifying themselves with omega-3 fatty acids.

Why all the fuss? The Latin name for shad means "fish most delicious," and fish devotees seem to agree about its delicate flavor, though some find the fish too bony to work with. Shad roe was called "one of the great delicacies of the world" by the late preeminent American chef James Beard, who preferred it smothered in butter with a touch of lemon.

Shad Festival:

Each April, Lambertville celebrates the return of the shad to the Delaware River.

you know you're in
new jersey when...
...there are shadows lurking in Shadow Lawn

Ooooooooooweeee . . . New Jersey may be the most haunted state in America, and that makes sense. We have lots of old buildings and farms reputed to be occupied by the spirits of pirates, colonial soldiers, and mysterious women. (And that doesn't include all those locations that wiseguys favored as places to dump people they whacked.) The formula for haunting seems to be this: The richer and more colorful the history, the likelier it is that a place is shrouded in tales of ghosts.

Certainly Shadow Lawn, once the site of Woodrow Wilson's summer White House, has had a past both rich and checkered. Though the original mansion burned in 1927, a replacement was built in 1929 for Woolworth Co. president Hubert T. Parson and his wife. Now part of Monmouth University, the residence is formally known as Woodrow Wilson Hall. Its ghostly history is captured in an hour-long documentary entitled *Shadows of Shadow Lawn,* made by Tom Hanley and Patrick Perrotto.

When the Parsons were in residence, there was a midnight curfew—perhaps for good reason. During an overnight visit the modern-day filmmakers started hearing noises as the curfew hour approached. Doors opened and closed, drafts came down the stairs, and there were sounds of furniture being moved. The men interpreted these phenomena as indications of the deceased occupants of Shadow Lawn settling in for the night.

In what is now the Lauren K. Woods Theater (also part of the university complex), a stable boy was killed and his girlfriend committed suicide. One afternoon Hanley smelled the strong odors of a stable there—hay and manure—before the temperature suddenly dropped, but only in a single area.

And in the Guggenheim Memorial Library across the street from Shadow Lawn, one-time resident Leonia Guggenheim has been seen floating up the grand staircase. Guggenheim's scent, it is said, lingers in what was her powder room.

Shadow Lawn:

This mansion, now known as Woodrow Wilson Hall on the University of Monmouth campus, is but one haunted place in Jersey.

Back in the 1930s, when Bing Crosby was the undisputed king of America's crooners, a skinny Hoboken kid with a bad complexion and a voice like warm silk was playing dive bars and musty clubs, carrying his own P.A. system to his gigs.

After a brief stint with The Hoboken Four, Francis Albert Sinatra got work with Harry James and recorded his first hit, "All or Nothing at All." Next he signed with the Tommy Dorsey band for the princely sum of $125 a week—and soon was discovered by legions of bobby soxers, who swooned and screamed "Frankeeee" (much as a later generation of fans would scream for the Beatles). After breaking his contract with Dorsey—with Mafia assistance, according to legend—Sinatra soared to stardom, not only as a singer but as a film actor.

After a vocal cord hemorrhage nearly ended his career, Sinatra fought for and got the role of Maggio in *From Here to Eternity,* which earned him an Oscar for Best Supporting Actor. Sinatra went on to give memorable performances in such films as *The Man with the Golden Arm, Suddenly, The Manchurian Candidate, The Detective, The First Deadly Sin,* and *Guys and Dolls.*

In the 1950s Sinatra conquered Vegas. He and his pals—Dean Martin, Sammy Davis Jr., Peter Lawford, Joey Bishop, and occasionally Shirley MacLaine—were known as

Sinatra, Frank:

Ol' Blue Eyes, The Voice, or the Chairman of the Board—whatever you call him, this Jersey Guy became a legend in his own time.

the Rat Pack. Though it was the Rat Pack's wacky antics that made headlines, they played an important part in desegregating Nevada's hotels and casinos by boycotting any place that refused service to Davis Jr.

From Sinatra's vocal canon, many fans most remember the lyrics that extol Chicago and New York. But Sinatra created a brash and sometimes swaggering persona, on screen and in life, that is pure Jersey Attitude, summed up in his signature song, "My Way."

you know you're in
new jersey when...

...a dead-end job at a convenience store leads to fame and fortune

Kevin Smith's story is the stuff of urban legend and an inspiration to budding directors everywhere. A dropout from both the New School for Social Research and the Vancouver Film School, the Highlands native went to work at a Quick Stop convenience store. The job proved to be far from dead end, for it gave him the inspiration for his first film, *Clerks.*

Smith funded the black-and-white film with credit cards, loans, insurance money from two cars destroyed during a flood, money from his parents, a partial tuition refund, and the sale of his comic book collection—all of which netted him a working budget of $27,000. With Scott Mosier, a friend from the Vancouver Film School, he began filming at night in the convenience store where he worked by day, using friends and local actors to keep costs down.

The film was first shown in 1994 at the Sundance Film Festival, where, after a very slow start, it got the attention of Miramax executives. *Clerks* became a success on the indie circuit and led to a successful career for Smith, whose other films include *Mallrats, Chasing Amy, Jersey Girl, Dogma, Jay and Silent Bob Strike Back,* and *Clerks II.* Scenes from *Chasing Amy* were shot in Victory Park in Rumson, and many Jersey locations, including St. James Church at Red Bank Catholic High School, appear in *Dogma.*

Smith, Kevin:

This Jersey native, a former convenience store clerk, made a cheap film and found fame and fortune.

In addition to writing, directing, and acting in films, Smith owns Jay and Silent Bob's Secret Stash (www.jayandsilentbob.com) at 35 Broad Street in Red Bank. This comic book store, stocked largely with merchandise related to Smith's films, is a treasure trove for fans. Stop by to browse the T-shirts and posters, some signed by the director himself.

you know you're in
new jersey when...
...a Soprano is definitely *not* going to sing

When the wildly popular HBO series about a dysfunctional crime family returned to the small screen in 2002, after a long hiatus, fans raced home to their 50-inch plasma televisions. Rutgers grad James Gandolfini is practically a demigod here in the Sopranos State, as it's been dubbed, and everything related to the show has achieved cult status.

Most natives recognize locales from *The Sopranos,* such as Pizzaland and the Muffler Man, but many out-of-staters need the Sopranos Tour offered by On Location Tours (www.sceneontv.com). Highlights include A. J.'s high school, Satriale's pork store, Big Pussy's auto repair shop, and, of course, the Bada Bing.

Tony Soprano and his world have become so real to viewers that the characters are actually "authoring" books, like *Entertaining with the Sopranos,* compiled by Carmela Soprano, and *The Sopranos Family Cookbook,* compiled by Artie Bucco.

Granted, Tony's Sunday dinner with the family always looks darn good, but applying his ethic to business seems a little scary. *Leadership Sopranos Style: How to Become a More Effective Boss* does not actually advocate whacking people, but it does praise Tony's "sit-downs" and his careful choice of team managers. Even more disturbing is *The Sopranos and Philosophy: I Kill Therefore I Am.*

Now, New Jersey certainly has its fair share of Italian-Americans—20 percent of the population, according to one estimate. Though most of us are *Sopranos* fans, a vocal minority is fed up with being portrayed as killers and thugs. Why don't people ever take notice of successful *paisans* like Supreme Court justices Antonin Scalia and Samuel Alito Jr.? they complain.

Sure, Jersey alone can claim wiseguys Anthony "Little Pussy" Russo, Anthony "Gaspipe" Casso, and *capo di capi* Vito Genovese, but does that mean you have to grovel respectfully whenever you meet someone whose name ends in a vowel? Sounds reasonable to us.

The Sopranos:

Love 'em or whack 'em, Jersey's favorite TV family is here to stay.

Imagine that you had ancestors who never threw anything away—antique cars and wagons, tools, toys, weapons, you name it. Add to that some 500 live animals, an Indian museum, and a huge stuffed bear, and you have some idea what the curious place known as Space Farms Zoo & Museum in Beemerville is like.

No, the "Space" part has nothing to do with outer space—it's simply a family name. The zoo started back in 1927, when Ralph and Elizabeth Space ran a small general store, gas station, and repair shop. Ralph supplemented the family's income by working for the state Game Department, trapping predators that threatened area farm animals. He caught bobcats, foxes, and raccoons—all of which his children wanted to keep.

Over time the menagerie grew, becoming the largest private collection of North American wildlife in the world. The zoo is now home to such exotics as lions, Bengal tigers, llamas, jaguars, and monkeys. Space Farms also takes part in programs to restore endangered species.

One enduring attraction is Goliath, a bear who died in 1991 but who lives on in the *Guinness Book of World Records* as the largest bear in the world. In life he weighed 2,000 pounds and stood 12 feet tall. Thanks to the wonders of taxidermy, he is still on display.

After visiting the animals, you might wend your way through the museum displays— 50,000 artifacts, including the cars, tools, weapons, et cetera that we previously mentioned. These collections started during the Great Depression, when folks around these parts traded their belongings for food from the general store.

Space Farms, still run by members of the Space family, is open daily May through October. Activities include wildlife demonstrations and discussions. For more information, visit www.spacefarms.com.

Space Farms:

This zoo and museum complex in Beemerville started with a part-time job in the late 1920s.

Let us make this perfectly clear: Although we've had plenty of beefs with New York, maybe even thought once or twice about sending Tony Soprano over to negotiate with grabby City politicians, we have never claimed that Lady Liberty belongs to Jersey—except in the sense that she belongs to all Americans.

Yes, we wish that Liberty Enlightening the World (her formal name) faced Jersey instead of showing us her back, but we have excellent ferries that allow us to say hello, face-to-face, any time we like. When France gave us the Bartholdi statue as a gesture of friendship and alliance, she was placed on what is now known as Liberty Island. Formerly Bedloe's Island, this piece of real estate was privately owned and later acquired—fair and square, we think—by the state of New York.

What we take exception to is New York's claim to the second part of the Liberty complex, Ellis Island. We know darn well that we have rights there, and former governor Christine Todd Whitman proved it through the Supreme Court in 1998. In a 6–3 vote, the justices ruled that most of Ellis Island—24.2 acres—is indeed in Jersey. Those acres have terrific head-on views of the statue! Great news, right?

Not exactly, to judge by public reaction. A lot of people said "Whatever," since no mat-

Statue of Liberty and Ellis Island:

Lady Liberty may belong to New York, but most of Ellis Island is technically part of New Jersey.

ter whose map it's on, Ellis Island is a national park owned by the federal government. Even worse, New Yorkers made fun of the fact that the museum and hall stand on their 3.3 acres—and that our 24.2 acres were basically the landfill used to expand the island in the late 19th century, when millions of immigrants were landing on American shores.

We think that New Yorkers miss the point. The issue isn't about land or landfill. It is, as former Jersey City mayor Brett Schundler once said, "really about respect."

you know you're in
new jersey when...
... the state's mineral riches leave you all aglow

In the 1800s prospectors out west cried, "There's gold in them thar hills!" Here in Jersey they said, "There's zinc up there!" Indeed, we had zinc aplenty.

The Sterling Hill Mine (named after William Alexander, Lord Stirling [sic]) in Ogdensburg and its sister mine in Franklin make up one of the most renowned mineral districts in the world. More than 340 minerals are found there—a world record for the number of mineral types in a single locale, and about 10 percent of all the earth's known minerals. About half of these minerals are found nowhere else in the world.

What is especially interesting, in addition to the richness of the ore, is that many of these minerals fluoresce. When the mines were electrified around the turn of the 20th century, equipment sparks gave off ultraviolet light, which revealed a spectacular fluorescent display.

Budding geologists might like to know that the ore mined from Sterling and Franklin was primarily zinc ore, which consists of the minerals known as zincite, franklinite, and willemite. The ore became part of cars, radios, and pharmaceuticals, to name just a few common things.

The Franklin Mine closed in 1954, and the Sterling Hill Mine followed in 1986; this brought an end to underground mining in Jersey. But if you have a yen to experience a real mine—without the danger and dirt—you can indulge that fantasy, as the Sterling Hill site is now a museum (www.sterling hill.org). There are 30 acres of indoor and outdoor displays and historic buildings, but the real excitement is underground. There you can see the shafts where miners toiled, feel the minerals, and walk through tunnels that lead to a spectacular cavern lit by fluorescent minerals.

Fluorescence, you'll learn at the museum, is part of our everyday lives. You can find it in computer monitors and TV screens; in fluorescent office lights; and in laundry detergents, where it makes clothes appear whiter than they really are.

Sterling Hill Mine:

This renowned mineral district, once a rich source of zinc ore, is now a mining museum.

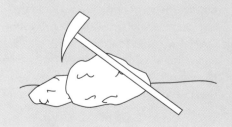

you know you're in
new jersey when...
...your garage band plays on the very stage where Springsteen became a legend

Though The Boss's early Asbury Park gigs took place at various clubs—including the Upstage and the Fast Lane—the Stone Pony is known as the club where Bruce made his musical bones.

Thanks in large part to Springsteen, the Pony is one of the best-known rock clubs in the world. Back in the 1970s, Southside Johnny and the Asbury Jukes was the house band at the Pony, which also attracted such stellar performers as Jon Bon Jovi, Cyndi Lauper, Elvis Costello, Greg Allman, and the Ramones over the years. Nowadays, it attracts movie stars, too: When Gladiator star Russell Crowe got his Australian band, 30 Odd Foot of Grunts, together, he told his agent that he wanted to play the stage where Springsteen played. And he did.

The Pony is much more pleasant than it used to be, thanks to an interior renovation and an outdoor stage. Check out the Web site (www.stoneponyonline.com), and you might see names like John Eddie (who traditionally opens the summer season), Nils Lofgren, and Clarence Clemons on the list of scheduled performers. When E Streeters like Lofgren and Clemons appear, Bruce-watchers fly to the box office, hoping The Boss will drop in, as he so often does.

Stone Pony:

This legendary club is closely associated with The Boss but has hosted scads of other talented performers as well.

Not all the musicians who appear at the Pony are famous. True to its roots, the club auditions local bands every season—so if you were born to rock and roll, contact the Pony at ponyrocks89@yahoo.com.

you know you're in
new jersey when...

... once upon a time is not so far away

About 10 miles west of Atlantic City, yet a world away from the clanging slots and neon lights, Storybook Land sweetly brings to life all the "Once upon a time . . ." stories of early childhood.

You'll find the Three Bears' house, invaded by Goldilocks; the Old Woman Who Lived in a Shoe (pre-Imelda); and giant likenesses of other fairy-tale characters. In all, there are more than 50 storybook buildings and displays that depict children's stories or nursery rhymes. Yes, there are a few concessions to modern technology—like the talking wolf that tries to fool Little Red Riding Hood—but they just add to the fun.

The 20-acre wooded park is clean and bright; there are no long lines, and there are no electronic games. Storybook Land is very popular with "legacies," adults who were brought here by their parents and grandparents and would like to relive a time of simpler pleasures with their own children. All those rosy-cheeked nursery-rhyme characters make for great photo ops.

Yes, Storybook Land is kitschy, but in a good way. Owned and operated by the Fricano family since it opened in 1955, the park is an antidote to high-priced, high-stress theme parks. The vintage rides are comfortable and nonthreatening for little kids—nothing here to make them (or you) nauseated—and picnic tables are available

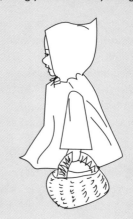

Storybook Land:

If you visit this park west of Atlantic City, bring your best storytelling voice.

for brown-bag lunches. All of this makes for a relaxing, relatively inexpensive day.

Storybook Land is also a place for happy holidays. At Halloween costumed kids can trick-or-treat in this safe environment, and thousands of lights illuminate the park during the Christmas season.

In Jersey-speak (and in many older Neapolitan restaurants), pizza is known as tomato pie. In fact, when we see a sign advertising tomato pies, we gain confidence that what we're about to eat is the real thing.

There are folks who like their pizza thick and doughy. While this might make for a cheap and filling lunch, tomato pie aficionados scorn such heavy-handed versions. For the true tomato pie lover, thin crust is paramount. That's because authentic pizza has its roots in 18th-century Naples, in a flatbread known as pita. The marinara version was topped with uncooked tomatoes, oregano, garlic, and olive oil. To celebrate the visit of Italy's Queen Margherita to Naples in 1889, the Margherita variation, with mozzarella and basil, was created.

So far we have a few basic ingredients. Yet in many places—free-thinking California, for example—pizza makers think it's perfectly okay to heap their pies with weird toppings, including various vegetables, ham, and even pineapple!

We deplore such innovation. Better to take after Jersey boy and master *pizzaolo* Anthony Mangieri, whose Una Pizza Napoletana originally was located in Point Pleasant. Mangieri gained fame and glowing reviews by making only the classics: Margherita; *filetti* (fresh cherry tomatoes, buffalo mozzarella, garlic, and basil with extra-virgin olive oil and sea salt); and *bianca* (white pizza with cheese and no tomatoes).

On his menu the chef states: ". . . all the square, round, thick, stuffed and overtopped pieces of dough may be to your liking, but don't call it pizza." We agree—heartily.

Although Mangieri relocated his restaurant to New York's East Village in October 2004, the authentic Neapolitan pie lives on at places like Federici's in Freehold, Vic's in Bradley Beach, and Pete and Elda's Bar in Neptune City. At the latter, a satisfied customer once raved that the pie was as "thin as a matzo."

Tomato Pie:

That's what Jersey natives call pizza—you got a problem with that?

you know you're in
new jersey when...
...the wheels on the bus go round and round... and round

In London they're called rotaries or round-abouts—tight little turning circles for itty-bitty cars. The more poetic Parisians call them *étoiles,* or stars. In fact, one of the City of Light's biggest tourist attractions is a vast, 12-pointed driver's nightmare called *Place de l'Etoile* (the famous Arc de Triomphe happens to occupy the center).

Tourists rarely come to Jersey to visit our traffic circles, but some have gained notoriety nonetheless. Locals dubbed the Routes 1 and 9 circle under the Pulaski Skyway in Jersey City "Crash Corner," for example.

The traffic circle is an old-fashioned way of creating an intersection of two or more highways without traffic lights or costly, view-obstructing overpasses. It did not originate here, but we certainly have more than any other state.

In fact, traffic circles are so peculiar to Jersey that they have become a litmus test to separate tourists from natives. If you're one of those flustered out-of-staters who provokes swearing and horn-honking, see yourself as we see you: SUV careening right at tip-over speed, then jerking back to your original lane without warning. Or maybe you're Timid Tilly, waiting until there are no cars anywhere in sight before proceeding.

If you insist on driving in Jersey, follow these tips for competent circumnavigation:

Know where you're going, and avoid sudden stops and lane changes. When you approach a circle, keep your eye on oncoming traffic and try to arrive at the merge when there's a gap. Practice your "Jersey stop," which is exactly like stopping except that your car keeps rolling (stick-shift drivers, stay in second gear). When you see an opening, hit the pedal on the right.

If you actually have your own lane and don't need to merge with oncoming traffic, then don't look for trouble, darn it. And unless you want a guided tour of the nearest ER, don't cut off other cars to make an exit. Remember, it's a traffic *circle*—you can go around again and get into the correct lane.

Traffic Circles:

New York's anti-gridlock slogan is "Don't block the box." In Jersey we say, "Don't be a circle jerk."

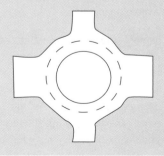

you know you're in
new jersey when...
... on a clear day you can see Tucker's Island

Longtime Garden State residents love to lament the disappearance of favorite places—Palisades Amusement Park, Mac's Embers Restaurant in Long Branch, and the Tradewinds Beach Club in Sea Bright. But not many people outside of Ocean County remember when an entire community disappeared.

If you have a large, very detailed map of New Jersey, you might see a small speck just south of Long Beach Island. This tiny patch of land is all that's left of Tucker's Island, one of the earliest resorts on the Jersey Shore. It was born during the winter of 1800, when heavy tides surged over the southern end of Long Beach Island and created a channel—now called Beach Haven Inlet—all the way through to Barnegat Bay.

Once a thriving community of year-rounders and seasonal visitors, Tucker's Island included Tucker's Beach, Sea Haven, and Short Beach. The area was originally 8 miles long, with homes, a school, and a U.S. Life Saving Service Station. It also hosted a lighthouse, a small one built in 1848 and replaced in 1879 by a bigger, better tower equipped with a fourth-order Fresnel lens.

By the turn of the 20th century, shifting tides had whittled Tucker's Island down to barely a mile, and by 1927 the ocean had undermined the lighthouse, which collapsed into the briny deep. The island fol-

Tucker's Island:

This 19th-century resort became the Atlantis of the Jersey Shore.

lowed suit. By 1955 it had been completely swallowed up by the sea—though it reappears when the tides are right.

The current residents of Long Beach Island love to fish, sail, and play in the ocean—but they take heed of the water's destructive power. The Long Beach Island Museum, located in Beach Haven's original church (Holy Innocents), includes dramatic photos of the demise of Tucker's Island.

At Tuckerton Seaport (www.tuckerton seaport.org), a 40-acre living-history museum dedicated to New Jersey's maritime heritage, you'll find a replica of the old Tucker's Island lighthouse, this one safely located on the mainland.

In 1804 New Jersey passed An Act for the Gradual Abolition of Slavery, which made the state a promised land for runaway slaves. In 1830 the term *Underground Railroad* came into use to describe a network of people and places that helped runaways from the South reach freedom in the North and in Canada.

It's estimated that between 30,000 and 50,000 slaves were helped to freedom by this network.

New Jersey was an important part of the system, receiving slaves from Delaware, Maryland, Virginia, the Carolinas, and Georgia.

New Jerseyan William Still, who worked for the Underground Railroad in Philadelphia, wrote a book titled *The Underground Railroad* in 1872, detailing the heroic struggles of the slaves who sought freedom. The legendary Harriet Tubman worked summers in Cape May hotels from 1849 to 1852 to finance her work in guiding slaves from her native Maryland to freedom in New Jersey; it's estimated that she assisted some 300 people.

No other northern state exceeded New Jersey in the number of all-black communities that served as refuges for fugitive slaves. Among these were Springtown in Cumberland County, Marshalltown in Salem County,

Underground Railroad:

New Jersey played a major role in helping runaway slaves to freedom.

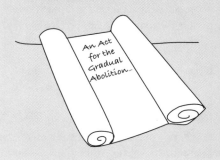

Snow Hill in Camden County, and Timbuctoo in Burlington County. Once they reached communities like these, the runaways were safe, and slave hunters who followed them were likely to be driven away.

Forget the $500 claimers at the Meadowlands. The stables at the United States Equestrian Team headquarters in Gladstone (www.uset.org) shelter some of the priciest horseflesh in the world. When these blue-bloods are not being put through their paces, training in show-jumping and dressage for international competitions like the Pan American Games or the Olympics, they get to cool down in one of the most luxurious stables in the United States.

Their home, Hamilton Farm, was the folly of Wall Street financier James Cox Brady, his rustic retreat away from the pressures of the city. Brady started with a small plot of 180 acres, bought at $100 an acre, and kept adding to it until his domain totaled 5,000 acres and sprawled over three counties. Construction began in 1911 and lasted until 1916. Brady named the estate, which cost more than $1 million, after his wife, Elizabeth Jane Hamilton Brady.

The tycoon kept all kinds of animals on his gentleman's farm, but his special interest was horses, which explains the lavish stable. Constructed of brick and concrete and reinforced with steel, it has an ornate interior that includes carriage rooms (now USET executive offices) and tack rooms with tile walls, terrazzo floors, and brass fittings. There are 54 box stalls with cork brick floors, which cushion the precious hooves and keep the surroundings quiet and soothing.

In the trophy room, which has glass-enclosed walnut cases, stained-glass ceiling lights, and oak flooring, are ribbons and awards that America's equestrian teams have won over the years.

Visits can be arranged by appointment (call 908–234–1251). A good time to see the property in all its glory is during the annual Gladstone Antiques Show in mid-September, when the 54 box stalls become booths for upscale antiques dealers.

USET Headquarters:

If this is how hayburners live in Jersey, then pass us the oats.

With a golf history that goes back to the 1890s, the Garden State has its share of the game's hallowed ground—more than 30 vintage tracks designed by Donald Ross, A. W. Tillinghast, and the lesser-known Charles "Steamshovel" Banks, in fact.

Most of these courses, including Shacka-maxon, Plainfield, Somerset Hills, Atlantic City County Club, and Baltrusol, are private and off-limits to the general public. Don't even ask how to get on Pine Valley; often rated the country's best golf course, it is also notoriously exclusive.

But one shrine to the game that welcomes all comers is the Golf House in Far Hills, home of the United States Golf Association (www.usga.org). The Golf House has the world's largest collection of golf memora-bilia, with artifacts dating back to the mid-1300s.

An entire room is devoted to the life and exploits of Bob Jones, but there are dis-plays about many other memorable golfers as well—from Mary, Queen of Scots, to Tiger Woods to golf-loving U.S. presi-dents—along with their clubs.

Among the museum's most famous exhibits is astronaut Alan Shepard's "moon club," the rigged-up six-iron he took aboard the *Apollo 14* in 1971. If you remember your history, Shepard's first one-handed swing

was actually a duff (okay, let's call it a prac-tice shot), but he connected on his second stroke, which he reported went for "miles and miles" on the moon's surface. He later changed his estimate to 200 to 400 yards. Good thing no one was actually keeping score.

Golf House is also equipped with a research and testing facility, where officials rule on the legality of the latest high-tech golf balls and behemoth drivers. Though visitors aren't permitted on the testing range or in the lab, there is an observation deck. Call 908–234–2300 for information on hours of operation, as the museum temporarily closed for renovations in 2005.

USGA Golf House:

Home to a museum as well as a testing and research facility, this shrine to golf is located in Far Hills.

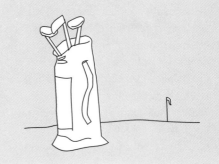

...bustles and high-button shoes are the latest fashions

During the dog days of summer, you'll see women wearing skimpy bikinis in Cape May. But come October, when the fine, crisp autumn weather fills the sea air, the resort reverts to its Victorian roots for 10 full days.

With some 600 beautifully restored structures representing every major architectural style of the Victorian era, Cape May is a virtual time capsule of this extravagant epoch. In fact, it is the only city in the United States designated a National Historic Landmark.

History comes alive during Victorian Week, when costumed ladies and gents promenade decorously down the tree-lined streets, past stately houses lavishly ornamented with columns, scrolls, lattices and fretwork, many authentically painted in a harmony of colors to make every detail stand out.

Cape May offers a full calendar of happenings that have fun with the Victorian theme. You can visit a historic house or hear a brass band play Sousa. Or perhaps an elegant horse-drawn barouche is waiting to whisk you to a period ball, where you'll dance a lively quadrille, a graceful waltz, or even a polkalike schottische.

Victorians-for-a-while get into the spirit of the period with such events as the Temperance Tantrums dinner. The host of the dinner is supposed to be Dr. Emlen Physick, a

Victorian Week:

Anyone in Cape May can be a Victorian for a day—but after that the corset's got to go.

19th-century gentleman farmer whose estate is now home to the Mid-Atlantic Center for the Arts. During the dinner, the good doctor is interrupted by members of the Eternal Sword Temperance Union. While the intruders rail against demon rum, the dinner guests are encouraged to enjoy a brew or two—and a boisterous good time is had by all.

Other popular events include ghost tours and sessions with a medium—Victorians were mad for Spiritualism. And since you brought your deerstalker cap, how about a little Sherlocking? At the traditional Murder Mystery dinners, everyone loves to solve a whodunit.

you know you're in
new jersey when...
...little green men take over your town

On Halloween night in 1938, millions of unsuspecting Americans tuned their radios to the Mercury Theater of the Air. The program that evening was to be an adaptation of H. G. Wells's science fiction novel *War of the Worlds,* which was about a Martian invasion of Earth.

Little did listeners know that producer/director Orson Welles had a surprise in store for them. To heighten the dramatic effect of the piece, Welles decided to have it performed as if an invasion were actually taking place.

As music played, a fake bulletin suddenly interrupted with the news that "a huge flaming object" had dropped onto a farm in Grovers Mill, New Jersey. Later, an announcer intoned that an alien was emerging from the spacecraft: "I can see the thing's body. It's large as a bear and it glistens like wet leather. But that face. It . . . it's indescribable. I can hardly force myself to keep looking at it. The eyes are black and gleam like a serpent. The mouth is V-shaped with saliva dripping from its rimless lips that seem to quiver and pulsate." And so it went.

Frightened out of their wits, people ran screaming from their homes and took to the roads. Some hid in their cellars, armed with guns and whatever they could lay hands on to repel the invaders. The panic

War of the Worlds:

Grovers Mill was the site of the original Martian invasion, but Bayonne and Howell served as locations for a 2005 movie version of the H. G. Wells classic.

caused a national scandal and generated scores of articles demanding that someone do something to prevent such a thing from happening again. After much ado, nothing was done—though Welles did express his regrets.

Reprising the Garden State connection for his 2005 film version of *War of the Worlds,* director Steven Spielberg shot a number of scenes in New Jersey locations, including Bayonne and Howell. As far as anyone knows, no New Jerseyans were harmed during the filming, nor did they take to the roads when they saw the movie.

...you celebrate Christmas by crossing the Delaware

Back in December 1776, there were no candy canes or Christmas stockings for General George Washington, whose poorly equipped Continental Army was decimated by defeats, disease, and desertion. Having already surrendered New York City to the almighty British Navy, Washington knew he had to defend Philadelphia at all costs.

Deciding to strike first, Washington set out on Christmas night, crossing the ice-choked Delaware River with 2,400 men, 16 boats, and 18 cannons. The party landed at Johnson's Ferry (now Washington Crossing State Park) at 4:00 A.M. on December 26. From there the troops marched on Trenton to attack the Hessians, who were doubtless a little worse for holiday cheer.

On January 2, 1777, at the second Battle of Trenton, Washington once again outmaneuvered the British forces. The next day the general reached Princeton and defeated the British rear guard. These were the first significant victories for the Continental Army, and they saved the American Revolution.

Every Christmas Day at Washington Crossing State Park in Titusville (609–737–0623), history buffs reenact Washington's 1776 crossing of the Delaware River, with volunteers in period costume carrying muskets and powder horns. Recent waves of patriotism have resulted in record crowds, making for a lively as well as educational outing.

At the visitor center you can watch films and view an extraordinary collection of Revolutionary War–era artifacts in the Swan Historical Foundation Collection. The Swans were a colonial family that saved everything from weapons to letters. Among their treasures are a piece of Washington's coffin and an example of the first American money, coined from Martha Washington's silver tea service.

On the park grounds is the Johnson Ferry House, an 18th-century farmhouse and tavern that Washington probably visited. If the urge to quick-march should overtake you, set out down the 1.5-mile Continental Lane toward Trenton; it's part of the route that Washington's army took in 1776.

Washington Crossing the Delaware:

This epochal moment in the American Revolution is reenacted each Christmas in Titusville.

you know you're in
new jersey when...
... the glassworks is at least half full

"Down in southern New Jersey, they make glass. By day and by night, the fires burn on in Millville, and bid the sand let in the light." The great American poet Carl Sandburg wrote that ode to our state's alchemic industry in his 1904 book *In Reckless Ecstasy.*

Though the 1888 factory is gone, the fires are still burning in Millville—and they are still making glass. At the T. C. Wheaton Glass factory, a working facility modeled after the old factory, glassblowers demonstrate their art and even assist visitors who would like to create an original paperweight as a souvenir. The factory is the centerpiece of Wheaton Village (www.wheaton village.org), a tribute to New Jersey's sober, pre-wiseguy days.

The Museum of American Glass, also in Wheaton Village, is the largest museum in the country dedicated to the history of American-made glass. A 2,000-book research library complements the exhibits, which include humble pieces that have historic value; stunning displays from Steuben and Tiffany; and the work of contemporary artists such as Paul J. Stankard, Dale Chihuly, and Ginny Ruffner. Don't miss curiosities such as the world's largest glass bottle. Made in the factory and featured in the *Guinness Book of World Records,* it is 7 feet, 8 inches tall and can hold 188 gallons of liquid.

The Wheaton complex includes Crafts and Trades Row, where potters, glassblowers, carvers, and tinsmiths create Jersey crafts; the 1876 one-room Centre Grove Schoolhouse, which also served as a church; and the Down Jersey Folklife Center, dedicated to preserving the heritage and traditions of south Jersey.

Given that museum visits often inspire a lust for shopping, the Gallery of American Craft offers a liberal helping of nostalgia along with merchandise ranging from penny candy to paperweights to exquisite glass Christmas ornaments.

Wheaton Village:

This crafts center in Millville offers educational exhibits about glassblowing as well as plenty of shopping opportunities.

you know you're in
new jersey when...
...you dine at the White House surrounded by celebrities and politicians

You won't get fine wines or crested china at Atlantic City's White House, but you're also not likely to encounter George W. Bush. Still, there are politicians aplenty; hundreds of photos lining the walls attest that this White House—a submarine sandwich shop at the corner of Arctic and Mississippi Avenues—is a popular photo-op for Garden State governors.

The "who's who" also includes boxers, singers, and actors, not to mention many smiling Miss Americas. You'll recognize Frank Sinatra, the Beatles, Joe DiMaggio, and Bruce Springsteen, but you may rack your brain trying to identify some of the more faded photos.

Now, this is no collection of generic head shots; many of the images were taken in the restaurant and/or personally inscribed. Some celebs, like the late Sinatra and Philadelphia native Bill Cosby, have even had White House subs flown out to them when the craving struck.

At lunchtime the line stretches out the door, so regulars call ahead. Gamblers, truckers, waitresses—everyone loves White House subs. Their Italian cold cuts are excellent, but the cheesesteak is the star. It's 91.1% fat-free USDA Choice top round, sliced thin and smothered in mushrooms, onions, tomatoes, and diced hot cherry peppers. The cheese is melted provolone, which has a nice, chewy texture and tangy

White House:
This Atlantic City sub shop serves cheesesteaks that could make Philly weep.

taste. It's all served on foot-and-a-half-long Italian bread from Formica's (pronounced "for-MEE-kuz") Bakery across the street, delivered several times a day so it's always fresh and fabulous.

Though the White House comprises only a lunch counter and half a dozen booths, it is not just some greasy spoon. The shop has received the James Beard Foundation Big Spoon award, given to "classic locally owned and operated restaurants beloved in their community." (The only other New Jersey restaurant so honored in 2000 was the very fancy Ryland Inn.) White House owner Anthony Basile didn't attend the awards ceremony, and manager Thomas Peterson doubted the award would change the restaurant or Mr. Basile, saying, "He's been the same for 50 years."

you know you're in
new jersey when...
... you don't tilt at WindMills, you eat at 'em

Paris can have its Moulin Rouge—you probably can't even get french fries there. New Jersey's WindMill, on the other hand, is *the* place for gourmet fast food: foot-long hot dogs, chargrilled burgers, deep-fried mushrooms with horseradish sauce, and hip-expanding cheese fries.

A fixture in Long Branch's West End, the original WindMill is a red-and-white cedar shake tower with blades gaily lit at night. For many of us who spent summers at the Jersey Shore, eating on the upstairs deck remains a vivid memory. Swarms of yellow jackets still circle the trash cans filled with discarded sodas. If this is not exactly your idea of fine dining, you can always take your meal a block away to the pedestrian boardwalk and enjoy it with an ocean view.

Over the years the WindMill has become a successful local franchise, expanding its range "up north" as far as Westfield, Summit, and Piscataway. You can even buy WindMill frankfurters at local supermarkets and share the love at your next backyard barbeque. If you have the talent and fortitude of a competitive eater, enter the annual WindMill Hot Dog Eating Contest in August. There's no charge for the dogs, but any antacids you require afterward are at your own expense.

WindMill:

The motto at this New Jersey hot dog haven is "Bigger! Better!"

With 10 locations throughout the Garden State, the WindMill guarantees that you're never far from your next wiener. Visit the company's Web site (www.windmillhotdogs .com) for addresses as well as a printable discount coupon and nifty hot dog trivia, such as these factoids: Babe Ruth once downed 24 hot dogs between games of a doubleheader, and Yankee Stadium sells more franks than any other ballpark, despite the Bambino's demise.

Cardinals, blue jays, and hundreds of other species are among those counted in the New Jersey Audubon Society's World Series of Birding, held every May in Cape May. Located at the southern end of the state, where the Delaware River meets the Atlantic Ocean, Cape May has long been recognized as one of the world's premier bird-watching spots.

The World Series, which has been timed to coincide with the annual spring migration, attracts bird-lovers from all over the world to witness thousands of birds passing through Cape May en route to their northern nesting grounds. Teams, individuals, youth/school groups, and novice backyard birders compete to identify as many different species as they can within a 24-hour period. A recent addition to the competition is the digiscope division, whereby the birds being observed are also photographed.

The entire Garden State is fair game, but teams must check in at Cape May Point State Park before the end of the 24-hour vigil. Teams usually average about 165 different species, but totals vary according to weather, skill, experience, fortitude, and just plain luck. Since 1984 more than 300 different species have been observed and officially recorded during the event.

A nice sidebar to this competition: Team members raise money for their favorite environmental causes by gathering pledges based on the number of birds they see. In 2005 more than $600,000 was raised. Find out more about this event and other birding get-togethers throughout the state by visiting www.njaudubon.org or calling (609) 884–2736.

World Series of Birding:

This annual bird-watching marathon in Cape May lets birders go cuckoo.

index

R'S SOURCE

With more than 100 Mid-Atlantic-related titles, we have the area covered. Whether you're looking for the path less traveled, a favorite place to eat, family-friendly fun, a breathtaking hike, or enchanting local attractions, our pages are filled with ideas to get you from one state to the next.

For a complete listing of all our titles, please visit our Web site at www.GlobePequot.com. The Globe Pequot Press is the largest publisher of local travel books in the United States and is a leading source for outdoor recreation guides.

FOR BOOKS TO THE MID-ATLANTIC

INSIDERS' GUIDE®

FALCON GUIDE®

Available wherever books are sold.
Orders can also be placed on the Web at www.GlobePequot.com,
by phone from 8:00 A.M. to 5:00 P.M. at 1-800-243-0495,
or by fax at 1-800-820-2329.